"Because you are reading t
connecting with God and
much and was deeply chal
As you immerse yourself

promise your journey will be extraordinary!"

—Tom McCoy, senior pastor,
Thompson Station Church

"The acronym of *SEEK*—surrender, exalt, expose, knock—is an ideal methodology for a lifestyle of prayer and intimacy with Jesus Christ. I highly implore you to read, and make use of, the rich and dynamic insights offered in her new book."

—Dr. Stephen Phinney, chancellor of Identity Matters Worldview
Institute and founder and ministry host of IOM America

"For decades, Jennifer Kennedy Dean has been leading in the area of prayer! She has knocked it out of the park again with her latest work *SEEK: 28 Days to Extraordinary Prayer*. I found her work trustworthy, stimulating, and fresh. I am enriched because I took twenty-eight days to *SEEK God in extraordinary prayer*. You will not be disappointed."

—Paul Covert, author, speaker, pastor of prayer development in
multiple churches, and prayer consultant

"Jennifer Kennedy Dean leads individuals, groups, and churches to God's heart as they learn to *SEEK*. We spent decades in church leadership, and transformation happens when individuals live a praying life. Our lives were positively impacted, and we believe yours will be too."

—Pam and Bill Farrel, codirectors of Love-Wise and authors of
numerous books including bestselling *Men Are Like Waffles, Women
Are Like Spaghetti* and *A Couple's Journey with God*

"Jennifer Kennedy Dean has always said, 'We don't have a prayer life, we live a praying life,' and through the Holy Spirit's leadership, she has given us yet another great tool to use in obtaining just that kind of life! Jennifer knows the Lord intimately and she so clearly reveals how we can have that intimacy as well. You don't want to miss this transforming opportunity. Make plans to start the journey today!"

—Mary Ann Bridgwater, Pray the Word Ministries

CHURCH AND PERSONAL STUDY RESOURCES FOR *SEEK*

Find resources to enhance your *SEEK* journey at
www.newhopepublishers.com/shop/seek
and
www.prayinglife.org

As a church, if you would like for *SEEK* to be part of a year of prayer,
you will find suggestions and resources to help you plan, including:

• Personal and small group reflection questions
• Sermon helps
• Sunday school lessons
• Artwork
• Video links
• And more

ABOUT THE AUTHOR

Jennifer Kennedy Dean is executive director of the Praying Life Foundation and a respected author and speaker. The author of numerous books, studies, and magazine articles specializing in prayer and spiritual formation, her Bible study *Live a Praying Life*® has been called a flagship work on prayer. Widely recognized as an unusually gifted communicator, Jennifer speaks all over the country calling God's people to discover the difference between a prayer life and a praying life. Jennifer is the author of such books as *Clothed with Power, Set Apart, Power in the Blood of Christ, Power in the Name of Jesus, Altar'd,* and *Secrets Jesus Shared.* Her engagements include respected organizations such as the Billy Graham Training Center at the Cove and Focus on the Family. She is a board member for Advanced Writers and Speakers Association, a member of America's National Prayer Committee, a member of National Professional Women Association, and national prayer director and board member for Christian Women in Media.

www.prayinglife.org
jennifer.k.dean.7
@prayinglife
@live_a_praying_life

SEEK

28 Days to Extraordinary Prayer

Jennifer Kennedy Dean

An imprint of Iron Stream Media
Birmingham, Alabama

New Hope® Publishers
5184 Caldwell Mill Rd.
St. 204-221
Hoover, AL 35244
NewHopePublishers.com
An imprint of Iron Stream Media

Library of Congress Cataloging-in-Publication Data

Names: Dean, Jennifer Kennedy, author.
Title: SEEK : 28 days to extraordinary prayer / Jennifer Kennedy Dean.
Description: First [edition]. | Birmingham : New Hope Publishers, 2019.
Identifiers: LCCN 2018053966 (print) | LCCN 2019002401 (ebook) | ISBN
 9781563091377 (Ebook) | ISBN 9781563091360 (permabind)
Subjects: LCSH: Prayer—Christianity.
Classification: LCC BV215 (ebook) | LCC BV215 .D3425 2019 (print) | DDC
 248.3/2—dc23
LC record available at https://lccn.loc.gov/2018053966

ISBN-13: 978-1-56309-136-0
Ebook ISBN: 978-1-56309-137-7

1 2 3 4 5—23 22 21 20 19

To my sons, daughters-in-law,
and grandchildren.
You are my rich treasure.

Other New Hope® Books
by Jennifer Kennedy Dean

CONTENTS

ACKNOWLEDGMENTS

Every book is a collaborative work. I want to thank all my readers who have been co-travelers with me on my long pursuit to understand prayer and to live in sync with the present-tense Jesus. Over the years, you have encouraged me, you have asked the probing questions that spurred me to go deeper, and you have shared your stories that made me rethink or reframe truth so that it is not static but living.

I thank all the staff at New Hope Publishers and Iron Stream Media for working with me to accomplish my vision and for being more than a publisher but also a partner in sharing the message.

AS YOU SEEK

As the deer pants for streams of water, so my soul pants for
you, my God. My soul thirsts for God, for the living God.
When can I go and meet with God? —Psalm 42:1

You, God, are my God, earnestly I seek you; I thirst for you,
my whole being longs for you, in a dry and parched land
where there is no water. —Psalm 63:1

Our souls cry out for God like our bodies cry out for water. Only
He can quench the places in our hearts where we are bone dry,
parched, desperate for His presence. At times, that ardent desire,
that acute need for Him, surfaces and everything we have turned to
previously—looking for what will fill our empty spaces—is proven
unsatisfying, its comfort fleeting.

Sometimes we have junctures in our lives at which our need for
His guidance is brought front and center. A momentous decision
or a significant life change or a new beginning—certain moments
in the flux of life's ebb and flow when the need that is always there
with us suddenly takes center stage and demands our attention. We
especially feel our utter helplessness and need of Him.

Sometimes in our walk with God, we just need a reboot.
A time comes when we realize our heart has become divided, and
we feel the pull of His voice calling us to regroup, to refocus, to
return. Nothing dramatic, perhaps. Just a longing to restore our

heart to its original design—to be His throne where He alone reigns. The shape of your prayer becomes:

> Teach me your way, LORD, that I may rely on your faithfulness; give me an undivided heart, that I may fear your name.
> —Psalm 86:11

This book is designed for those times when the weightiness of your need to hear from God and to receive His wisdom and guidance presses in on you, when your heart cries out to hear Him. When you are determined to attune your heart to His voice and your one goal becomes, "Speak, for your servant is listening" (1 Samuel 3:10).

> If you call out for insight and cry aloud for understanding, and if you look for it as for silver and search for it as for hidden treasure, then you will understand the fear of the LORD and find the knowledge of God. For the LORD gives wisdom; from his mouth come knowledge and understanding.
> —Proverbs 2:3–6

Heart Wide Open

Prayer is how we open our lives to God's power and provision, how we position our hearts to receive the outpouring of His wisdom and guidance, and how we offer our lives to be malleable in His hands so He can shape and mold us. Prayer is the artery connecting our hearts to God's so His life can flow into us and then through us.

> Prayer is the artery connecting our hearts to God's so His life can flow into us and then through us.

We limit prayer when we think of it as the means by which we can convince God of our point of view or talk Him into imparting something He is reluctant to give. When we view prayer as the method for influencing God to do our bidding, we miss its power.

As you embark on this twenty-eight day prayer encounter, settle in your mind and heart the purpose of your pursuit: to encounter Him, to hear His voice, and to find Him as your heart's true desire.

I say to the LORD, "You are my LORD; apart from you I have no good thing." —Psalm 16:2

Whom have I in heaven but you? And earth has nothing I desire besides you. —Psalm 73:25

SEEK

For all the many years of my ministry, I have had one message: We don't *have a prayer life,* we *live a praying life.* Prayer is more than an activity or a set of words packaged between "Dear God" and "Amen." Prayer is living in the continual flow of His power and provision, authored and nourished by the living, present-tense, indwelling Jesus. Once Jesus takes up residence in you, He is 24-7. He has moved in lock, stock, and barrel. All of Him in all of you. He does not move in and out. He indwells you, relentless in His love and single-minded in His determination to bring you into the abundant life He paid so high a price for you to possess. The fact that you have set your heart to seek Him is a response to His love that seeks you out and pulls

> Prayer is living in the continual flow of His power and provision, authored and nourished by the living, present-tense, indwelling Jesus.

you in. The love you feel toward Him is but an echo of the love He has for you.

In spite of the fact that I have had one message all these years, that message keeps unfolding, and my understanding of it keeps expanding. I grow daily in my walk of learning how to live a praying life. In this resource I hope to condense the concepts into a simple and palatable format that will challenge you and give you a structure for this twenty-eight-day pursuit and make it easy to take this journey in community with others. Since I have been writing and teaching on prayer for more than thirty years, I'll be drawing heavily on my previous writings as I unpack what Scripture has to say about living praying lives.

In spite of the fact that we live praying lives and always live in the flow of His presence, we undergird and nourish our praying lives through the daily discipline of focused prayer. This guide will give you some thoughts to lead you into that daily discipline of focused prayer.

To that end, we will concentrate on four pillars of prayer for which **SEEK** is an acronym. We will take one pillar each week and really get it kneaded into our hearts. The four areas of prayer are as follows:

SURRENDER

Yet you, LORD, are our Father. We are the clay, you are the potter; we are all the work of your hand. —Isaiah 64:8

Learn the power of relinquishment and the peace that comes with yielding.

Exalt

Glorify the LORD with me; let us exalt his name together.
—Psalm 34:3

Focus on the attributes of God in worship and adoration.

Expose

Search me, God, and know my heart; test me and know my
anxious thoughts. See if there is any offensive way in me, and
lead me in the way everlasting. —Psalm 139:23–24

Expose your heart to His Spirit and be open to His course
correction.

Knock

Ask and it will be given to you; seek and you will find; knock
and the door will be opened to you. For everyone who asks
receives; the one who seeks finds; and to the one who knocks,
the door will be opened. —Matthew 7:7–8

Turn to God with your needs and desires, anticipating His
perfectly timed and perfectly designed provision.

SURRENDER

Yet you, LORD, are our Father. We are the clay,
you are the potter; we are all the work of your
hand. —Isaiah 64:8

DAY 1

Surrender. Yield. Relinquish. These words do not hold a natural attraction for us. In fact, the opposite is often true. These words sound weak. Yet *surrender* is the first key to opening our hearts to God's voice and to His ways. So let's examine how what seems like weakness is really strength.

Let's be honest. Does prayer sometimes feel like a wrestling match? Do you find yourself approaching prayer as though its purpose is to win God over? As though you need to plead your case and convince God to act? Does it feel like you are trying to talk God into something?

Let's flip the script. Consider this: Prayer is not a way for you to influence God but a way for God to influence you. God does not have to be convinced to give. Giving is in His nature. He is more ready to give than you are to ask. He does not have to be encouraged to act in your best interest. You are the apple of His eye.

Reframe the purpose of prayer. Prayer is the way you open your heart toward God so He can do what only He can do. Seek Him for what He will do *in you*, not just for what He will do *for you.*

> Seek Him for what He will do *in you*, not just for what He will do *for you*.

This refocusing does not preclude Him working on your behalf in response to prayer. He will. He wants to. Scripture reminds us, "For the eyes of the Lord move to and fro throughout the earth that He may strongly support those whose heart is completely His" (2 Chronicles 16:9 NASB). We'll talk more about the power of asking when we get to the section on knocking. I just want you to see that the request aspect of prayer is not the whole picture. When we boil prayer down to only trying to get God to perform for us, then we miss out on the primary objective of prayer, and we never find the kind of peace and purpose God intends for prayer to provide.

In prayer, we make ourselves fully available to our heavenly Father, allowing Him access to every fragment of our being, every detail of our lives. Prayer flows out of His deep work in us.

> Consider a sponge. It has a molecular makeup that predisposes it to be absorbent. When a sponge comes into contact with a liquid, the sponge soaks up all of the liquid it can hold. That's just the nature of a sponge. A sponge, because of its design, can't keep from absorbing liquid. A sponge that has come into contact with liquid becomes saturated with that liquid. Everything about the liquid—all its chemical components and its color and smell and taste—is now soaked into the sponge. The sponge is the container of the liquid.
>
> When we were born again and became new creations, we were given a spiritual makeup that, when we come into contact with the living God, will absorb as much of Him as we can hold. His thoughts will transform our thoughts. His heart will reform our hearts. His desires will reshape our desires. We can partake of the divine nature. We have the mind of Christ. The Spirit reveals the deep things of God.
>
> As God authors our prayers, He doesn't just dictate to us. He changes us. As we purposefully keep our lives soaked in His presence, He will give *Himself* to us. —*Live a Praying Life® Workbook (10th Anniversary Edition),* pp. 70–71, emphasis added

Breathe

When I approach prayer as first the coming together of my heart
and His, as the releasing of all I am to all He is, it changes my experience of prayer. Prayer is not a duty to perform or simply a discipline to engage in, but rather prayer becomes the breath of my soul.

> Father, as I soak myself in Your presence, saturate me with
> Yourself. Seep into my spirit pores until I am filled with You.
> Let me breathe in Your love for me, and breathe it out again
> toward You. You are my treasure, and my heart knows no
> other home. —*Conversations With the Most High: 365 Days
> in God's Presence*, p. 139

Marinate Your Heart

Today in your designated time of prayer, focus on letting His desire
for relationship with you foment a response from your heart. What
does it mean to you right now that the God whose presence you
seek, seeks you? Write out your response in the space provided on
the next page.

In the quiet of the moment, in the inner sanctuary of your
own soul, allow yourself to feel loved. Even adored. Let your heart
soak in the words of Zephaniah 3:17. Pause after each phrase, and
let the truth put down roots.

> The LORD your God is with you, the Mighty Warrior who
> saves. He will take great delight in you; in his love he will no
> longer rebuke you, but will rejoice over you with singing.
> —Zephaniah 3:17

DAY 2

What exactly does it mean to surrender? *Webster's Dictionary* gives as one definition, "to give oneself up into the power of another." Surrender is a choice. It is a choice born from the alchemy of two truths: who I am and who He is.

> The beginning point of every prayer of faith is the prayer of relinquishment. . . . This is not a prayer of resignation to the circumstances; it's not throwing in the towel and giving up. The prayer of relinquishment can only come from a heart that knows the heart of the Father-Shepherd. We can abandon ourselves fully to His will because we know that His heart does not contain one thought or desire toward us that is anything less than the highest possible good.
>
> The prayer of relinquishment is the highest expression of full and mature faith in the Father. It is the truest experience of dying to your flesh in order to live by the Spirit. It is handing over control to the One who is worthy of such trust. The prayer of relinquishment is a statement of absolute surrender. This has become my prayer of relinquishment. *"Father, glorify your name"* (John 12:28). —*Live a Praying Life® Workbook (10th Anniversary Edition)*, p. 163

Who I Am, Who God Is

In thinking about who I am, perhaps I should start with who I am not. Everything that I am not, God is. Where I am limited, He is unlimited.

I Am Not All Wise

For the foolishness of God is wiser than human wisdom, and
the weakness of God is stronger than human strength.
—1 Corinthians 1:25

God Is All Wise

To God belong wisdom and power; counsel and understanding are his. —Job 12:13

I Am Not All Knowing

Trust in the LORD with all your heart and lean not on your
own understanding; in all your ways submit to him, and he
will make your paths straight. —Proverbs 3:5–6

God Is All Knowing

From heaven the LORD looks down and sees all mankind;
from his dwelling place he watches all who live on earth—
he who forms the hearts of all, who considers everything
they do. —Psalm 33:13–15

Nothing in all creation is hidden from God's sight. Everything
is uncovered and laid bare before the eyes of him to whom we
must give account. —Hebrews 4:13

I Do Not Have an Uncluttered Heart and Pure Motives

The heart is deceitful above all things and beyond cure. Who can understand it? —Jeremiah 17:9

God Does Have an Uncluttered Heart and Pure Motives

"For I know the plans I have for you," declares the LORD, "plans to prosper you and not to harm you, plans to give you hope and a future." —Jeremiah 29:11

I will rejoice in doing them good and will assuredly plant them in this land with all my heart and soul —Jeremiah 32:41

I Do Not Have an Eternal View

For who knows what is good for a person in life, during the few and meaningless days they pass through like a shadow? Who can tell them what will happen under the sun after they are gone? —Ecclesiastes 6:12

God Does Have an Eternal View

A thousand years in your sight are like a day that has just gone by, or like a watch in the night —Psalm 90:4

Remember the former things, those of long ago; I am God, and there is no other; I am God, and there is none like me. I make known the end from the beginning, from ancient times, what is still to come. I say, "My purpose will stand, and I will do all that I please." —Isaiah 46:9–10

Let God Be God

How much stress and anxiety, how many sleepless nights, how many emotional outbursts . . . how much upheaval in our hearts and relationships is the result of trying to do God's job for Him?

Father, today I exchange every worrying thought for thanksgiving. If the situations that worry me were indeed my responsibility—if You were looking to me to solve the problems and unravel the messes—then worry would make perfect sense. I'm not up to the job. I haven't a clue about how to resolve things. You are not depending on me for the answers. I'm looking to You for the answers. Thanksgiving and praise make more sense than worry. I acknowledge that all my stressing and worrying does not change anything except my state of mind. When I could be delighting in You and Your care, instead worry loads me down and steals all my joy. Today, I choose joy. —*Conversations With the Most High: 365 Days in God's Presence,* pp. 39–40

It is in our nature to want to be in control and try
outcomes. It is hard work, this trying to be in contro.
no peace to be found in trying to govern the ungovern
attempting to run the show. It is getting us nowhere. We j   ᴊpin
our wheels and expend energy without any forward momentum.
Jesus puts it this way, "The flesh [human effort] profits nothing"
(John 6:63 NASB). It accomplishes nothing; it moves nothing forward; it gives no benefit; it adds no value. The flesh profits nothing.

So surrender. You lose nothing by surrendering—to His plan,
His power, His wisdom, His process. You only gain. You gain
peace and perspective. You gain clarity and comfort. Let go.

Marinate Your Heart

Let your heart soak in the truths of the following Scripture passages. Even if the words are familiar, let your heart hear them afresh.
Stop after each phrase, and let the Holy Spirit apply it directly to
your life and your current circumstances. Write out your thoughts.

So do not fear, for I am with you; do not be dismayed, for
I am your God. I will strengthen you and help you; I will
uphold you with my righteous right hand. —Isaiah 41:10

I will make rivers flow on barren heights, and springs within
the valleys. I will turn the desert into pools of water, and the
parched ground into springs. —v. 18

DAY 3

With surrender comes rest. God does not intend for us to live with our emotions in chaos. He does not intend for our emotions to be our master. Think how easily your emotions can get the upper hand. Fear, resentment, frustration, anger, hurt, anxiety. When the events of our lives or the actions and

> God does not intend for us to live with our emotions in chaos. He does not intend for our emotions to be our master.

attitudes of people around us are outside of our control, it stirs up our flesh. Flesh is that aspect of your personality that is still acting in its own power rather than being the conduit of the Holy Spirit's power. Remember Jesus' words: "The flesh profits nothing."

Our flesh likes to be in control. Of everything. In control of ourselves, in control of the people around us, in control of our circumstances, in control of other people's circumstances. Nothing will throw our flesh into a bigger revolt than when we realize we have to hand over control. It's a death blow to our pride.

No way around it. Out-of-control flesh is the secret to surrendering to the power of the Spirit. Remember, there will be no shared governing. Flesh or Spirit, but not both.

When you are experiencing frustration, anger, or bitterness because you can't get the people around you to act like you need them to act, you can call that flesh. When you are in a panic, or filled with resentment because you can't manipulate circumstances into order, you can call that flesh.

The impulse of our flesh is to try harder, manage more, enforce our will more stringently, maneuver and massage and finesse until we get everyone and everything straightened out and marching to our beat. . . .

The reason that our flesh rises up and gives its all to make things fit its goals is because flesh promises that if everything and everyone would just do and be what we want them to do and be, then the happiness and peace that eludes us would be ours. Flimflam flesh. Big claims, no results. It gets you nowhere. —*Altar'd: Experience the Power of Resurrection*, p. 22

As you ponder what surrender means to you right now in the context of your present circumstances, do you recognize any flesh? Do you observe flesh-born emotions dictating your attitude? This is not a scold. This is a challenge to meet reality head-on and let the Holy Spirit work freedom into your heart. When I diagnose flesh and surrender that flesh on the altar, then I find that freedom begins to make inroads in my life.

Galatians 5:1 says, "It is for freedom that Christ has set us free. Stand firm, then, and do not let yourselves be burdened again by a yoke of slavery." I know Paul is specifically talking about not going back to depending on the law, but the principle is applicable. Don't let anything you previously put trust in—like your own flesh—rob you of the freedom Christ purchased for you.

Jesus' all-encompassing love for you means He will not relent and let flesh rule you. Freedom is His goal for you. Letting flesh flourish in your life and giving it room to operate diminishes, restricts, and robs you of the full, abundant life you are destined and designed for. So right now, when the Holy Spirit is nudging you and drawing you and challenging you to surrender, it is because He is zealous for you. He will not sit by and watch while you wrestle with the emotions that hold you hostage. Jesus said, "If you hold to my teaching, you are really my disciples. Then you will know the truth, and the truth will set you free" (John 8:31–32). When you *know*—understand, perceive, recognize, embrace—His truth, then that very truth will set you free. When we recognize we are ruled by our flesh and its emotions, that is the tip-off we are not living the truth. Surrender will be the turning point.

Needy

> The Creator designed us to have needs. He built needs into the blueprint so that those needs would be His entry points into our lives. He configured our needs so that they would be an exact match to His provision, as if the two were interlocking parts, fitting together hand-in-glove. Flesh takes those God-designed needs and tries to find their fulfillment on its own, from something or someone other than God.
> —*Altar'd: Experience the Power of Resurrection,* p. 30

God wants to meet your needs and fulfill your heart's desire. He designed the relationship so He could do so and thereby display His love for you and His power and ability. You don't have to convince Him.

What is robbing you of peace right now? What need or desire are you feeling some anxiety about or experiencing the frustration of not being able to make things line up with your expectations? Where are you trying to do for yourself what God wants to do for you? Stop and process it until you can pinpoint precisely where flesh is producing emotions and hijacking peace. Ask the Holy Spirit to reveal to you whatever you need to understand. Write out your observations.

As you clarify where you are out of alignment with His truth, lay each emotion and the situation that is producing it on the altar. As you do, beside where you have recorded that situation or emotion, write "YOURS." Feel the release. Welcome the freedom. Spend some time here. Let the relinquishment put down roots. Consider writing today's date beside your entries.

Marinate Your Heart

Hear the present Jesus speak Matthew 11:28 to you right now through His Holy Spirit. Respond.

> Come to me, all you who are weary and burdened, and I will give you rest. —Matthew 11:28

DAY 4

Yield. Abdicate ownership. Release. Take your hands off.

You have been listening to the Spirit bring to mind and identify where in your life you are maintaining ownership and trying to bring to heel the circumstances and relationships you are finally realizing will never be under your control.

Perhaps the content of your prayers has been centered on these concerns, pleading with God to do what you think should be done, how you think it should be done, when you think it should be done. This experience may be causing you to lose confidence in prayer's effect. You are worn down by your effort.

Right now, hear His gentle invitation to peace through surrender. You are not surrendering the outcome to your enemy. You are surrendering your effort to bring about the outcome you anticipate. This does not mean you stop praying in faith and expectancy. We'll look at that in the section on knocking. But our hearts have to be at a place of resting in God's perfect plan, even if that plan does not seem to line up with our calculations or our forecasted expectation.

Who can fathom the Spirit of the LORD, or instruct the LORD as his counselor? —Isaiah 40:13

"For my thoughts are not your thoughts, neither are your ways my ways," declares the LORD. "As the heavens are higher than the earth, so are my ways higher than your ways and my thoughts than your thoughts." —Isaiah 55:8–9

Praying with expectation is praying with our heart set on our best idea. Praying with expectancy is praying with the certainty that God is working on our behalf and that He is working out details we aren't even aware of. It is knowing He will come through at the perfect time in the perfect way. Praying with expectancy, at its core, is some variation on these words: Not my will, but Yours be done.

> Often we can have an underlying sense that God's will is something we have to bear up under or settle for. God's will, we think, is difficult and oppressive. In Romans 12:2, Paul described God's will with three words: good, pleasing, and perfect. Greek words used might be translated "beneficial," "bringing pleasure," and "a perfect fit." . . .
>
> Once you know for yourself that God's will is desirable, you will be able to trust that His will for all situations is equally desirable. You will learn to pray with expectant joy, let "your kingdom come, your will be done, on earth as it is in heaven" (Matthew 6:10). You will rest in His will completely.
>
> You can live at rest when the attitude of your heart becomes, "He is the LORD; let him do what is good in his eyes" (1 Samuel 3:18). This thought is echoed by Jesus. "Yes, Father, for this way was well-pleasing in Your sight" (Matthew 11:26 NASB).
> —*Synced: Living Connected to the Heart of Jesus,* pp. 115–116

Be Still

"Be still and know that I am God" (Psalm 46:10). I imagine you know these words and have heard them many times, but let's drill down into what God is really inviting us to.

The context of the psalm proclaims God's power and victory over every enemy. Because of that victory, His people can be still and know He wins the day every day. So settle down, quit striving, and be at rest. Why? Because He is God. He is loving and benevolent; He is all-knowing and all-wise; He is all-powerful; He is ever present everywhere. I AM is His name.

> Jesus lived out His life on earth with His soul at rest because He knew His Father had covered all the bases. All He had to do in times that might have caused fear and stress was to sync His heart to the Father's. Jesus walked naturally in the flow of His Father's peace. . . . He had to battle to a place of peace sometimes. But once there, He walked in it and it emanated from Him as His natural state. —*Synced*: *Living Connected to the Heart of Jesus*, p. 64

To surrender and live at rest does not mean to be passive. In fact, it means the opposite. When your swirling emotions are ruling, then you are less effective. God wants you to live a life of impact, a life through which His power freely flows. When you come to the place where you can relinquish everything that concerns you—hand it over to the One who has all power and provision—then you can act and respond from a center of strength and confidence.

Marinate Your Heart

Let your heart soak in the truth of Psalm 139:1–6. Ponder it word-by-word and phrase-by-phrase. Respond.

> You have searched me, LORD, and you know me. You know when I sit and when I rise; you perceive my thoughts from afar. You discern my going out and my lying down; you are familiar with all my ways. Before a word is on my tongue you, LORD, know it completely. You hem me in behind and before, and you lay your hand upon me. Such knowledge is too wonderful for me, too lofty for me to attain. —Psalm 139:1–6

DAY 5

The key to prayer—real prayer, not simply giving God a to-do list or mouthing rote words or trying to package the correct words between "Dear God" and "Amen"—is giving God full access to your heart. You already have full access to His. He is so willing to maximize your life and give you everything you need for living an amplified life that He gave His only Son.

> He who did not spare his own Son, but gave him up for us all—how will he not also, along with him, graciously *give us all things*? —Romans 8:32, emphasis added

Nothing held back. There is no selfishness in God. He gives because He is a giver. It is His nature. He wants to give more than you ask.

> He wants to give more than you ask.

> Now to him who is able to do *immeasurably more* than all we *ask or imagine*. —Ephesians 3:20, emphasis added

> And God is able to bless you abundantly, so that *in all things at all times*, having all that you need, you will abound in every good work. —2 Corinthians 9:8, emphasis added

When you say to God, "I'm all Yours. Everything I am and everything I have. All Yours," then you have opened your life to His *immeasurably more.* Yielding to Him and His plans and desires for you is not losing yourself. It is finding yourself. He is not withholding from you. He is doing everything possible to flood you with His abundance.

> In living a praying life, God's will is so exactly reproduced in us that it becomes our will. We find that when we pray the deepest desires of our hearts, we are stating His desires.
>
> The key to being able to receive all that God longs to give is to have a heart that is fully His. When His desires are in our hearts, His words rise from us as prayer. Our job is to allow the Spirit of God the access He needs to each of our hearts so He can cleanse them of debris. The clutter in our hearts throws off its acoustics. *Acoustics* are defined as "the qualities that determine the ability of an enclosure to reflect sound waves in such a way as to produce distinct hearing." How are your heart's acoustics? Does God need to do some renovation? Does He need to tear down some walls? Clear out some rubbish? Haul away some wreckage? Clean out some corners? —*Live a Praying Life® Workbook (10th Anniversary Edition),* p. 65

As we surrender to His love and cease all our turbulent trying, we find peace. Not peace induced by outward circumstances lining up as we thought they should but rather peace that comes from knowing in our inmost being that the Father is willing and ready to take the helm and direct every detail to its optimum outcome. To bring into and produce in our lives what He knows will accomplish our destiny and our fulfillment. He created us with a driving need to be happy. But happiness is the byproduct of holiness. Holiness means being set aside for God's purposes. Living surrendered. We will not find the happiness we are seeking unless we understand that our happiness is the blessedness found in holiness.

> We are able to live in the state of blessedness that God has created for us when we discover the key to true holiness. Rather than an uphill climb or a crushing burden, the call to holiness is a call to freedom and joy. We were made for holiness, and holiness is the best fit for our lives. We have been set apart by God, and we are grace-shaped. Only holiness fits us.
>
> The promise is not happiness, but blessedness. Happiness is transitory and driven by circumstance while blessedness is eternal and grounded in the reality of Christ in you. Blessedness leads to true happiness because, when viewed through the eternal grid, circumstances lose their power to toss your emotions around "like a wave driven by the wind."
> —*Set Apart: A Six-Week Study of the Beatitudes*, pp. 45–46

Soul Sabbath

The Hebrew word translated "Sabbath" (*šabbāṯ*) is from the root *šāṯaṯ*, meaning "to cease," "to desist," "to be finished." On the first Sabbath day, Scripture records that God rested (*šāṯaṯ*). When God established the Sabbath day, it was meant to serve also as a picture of the state of our souls.

> Sabbath for you and me means living our lives in absolute surrender and total trust in the finished work of Christ. Not only is the salvation work finished in Him but every need that comes into our lives has already been provided for, every dilemma has already been resolved, every question has already been answered. We simply have to place our lives in the flow of His provision. Simply abide in Christ. Simply live

where the power is operating. Hear Him say, "Come to Me. You will find rest for your soul." . . .

In the Gospel accounts, we see Jesus living in chaotic situations with life roiling around Him, but His heart is at rest. His bearing is calm and kind and patient. Unruffled in conflict, steady in unexpected situations, gentle with the broken, kind to the harsh. His peace comes from knowing that He is in the Father's care. That every moment is fully supplied by His loving Father. —*Synced: Living Connected to the Heart of Jesus*, pp. 64–65

Trade in your turmoil for His peace. Exchange your striving for His rest. Release your worry to His calm. Give up your anxiety for His confidence. It's all about the surrender.

Marinate Your Heart

Let your heart soak in the truths of Isaiah 26:3. Consider each word and phrase, and let the words take root. Respond.

You will keep in perfect peace those whose minds are steadfast, because they trust in you. —Isaiah 26:3

DAY 6

We like to see immediate results. We like for cause to produce effect. We like streamlined and efficient. We like to push a button and get what we are after.

But prayer doesn't work that way. By God's purposeful design, prayer has waiting periods. Those waiting periods have purpose behind them. If prayer would work best by operating like a vending machine—put in a prayer, get out an answer—then that's how prayer would work. But it doesn't.

God has designed prayer as a process, not an activity. He is doing more than we are praying for. In surrender, we are cooperating with the work He is doing *in us*, not just *for us*.

> God works through the prayer process to expand our vision, to deepen our hunger, to stretch our faith, and to lift our desires higher. We start the process desiring something from Him; we end it desiring only Him. Through the prayer process, our heart's cry becomes, "Whom have I in heaven but you? And earth has nothing I desire besides you. My flesh and my heart may fail, but God is the strength of my heart and my portion forever" (Psalm 73:25–26).
>
> When the Prayer Teacher has been able to reveal to you that He is all, that there is nothing to crave but more of Him, then you realize that He is willing to answer every prayer with a "yes"—because the heart of every true prayer is: "More of You. More of You." Your need or your desire is simply the entry point for Him to give you more of Himself. In meeting your need and

31

fulfilling your desire, He is drawing you to deeper dependence on Him, therefore to deeper intimacy with Him. —*Live a Praying Life® Workbook (10th Anniversary Edition)*, p. 76

When we have set out hearts on an expected outcome rather than on Him, we are not fully open to His work. We have a narrowed field of vision, and His works in response to prayer may well fall outside the tight, narrow focus of our expectations. Surrender means not living by belief in an outcome but by faith in God.

Weaklings

As we move to that place of absolute surrender, of deeper trust, of greater faith, then we are headed for the life God has designed. A life of walking in provision, living at rest, following the adventurous course God has set out for us.

As we recognize and own our weakness, we discover His strength in us. Our strength, at its peak, is pretty puny. Scripture says, "For the foolishness of God is wiser than human wisdom, and the weakness of God is stronger than human strength" (1 Corinthians 1:25). God is not trying to make you stronger. He is trying to get you out of the way so His strength can work through you.

> As we recognize and own our weakness, we discover His strength in us.

Therefore I will boast all the more gladly about my weaknesses, so that Christ's power may rest on me. That is why, for Christ's sake, I delight in weaknesses, in insults, in hardships, in persecutions, in difficulties. For when I am weak, *then I am strong.* —2 Corinthians 12:9–10, emphasis added

Observe what Jesus taught about strength through weakness in Matthew 5:3. When Jesus preached His first substantive sermon, what we call the Sermon on the Mount, He declared what He knew to be the foundation of kingdom living.

> Here He is, the new rabbi. The subject of all the buzz. This was apparently His first big gathering and His first substantive address, though He had been teaching in their synagogues. What would He say? How would He use His new notoriety? What agenda would He push? Would He razzle-dazzle them? Would He scold and rant?
>
> His first words were these: "Blessed are the poor in spirit, for theirs is the kingdom of heaven" (Matthew 5:3).
>
> The Greek word that is translated as "poor" is a word that implies being destitute, with no ability to provide for themselves, completely dependent on others to supply their needs. A beggar. He could have used a less stark word that would mean the working poor, those who just got by day to day. Instead, He used a word that meant utterly, abjectly impoverished.
>
> The very first thing He wanted to say about the new kingdom was that it belonged to those who recognized that they were incapable of providing spiritually for themselves. They brought nothing with them that would gain them entrance to the kingdom. They could do nothing that would give them stature in the kingdom. They could only possess the kingdom by receiving all from the hand of another.
>
> This is the foundational law for how the kingdom works. Everything else will build on this. Being poor in spirit is not just the way into the kingdom, but it is the way of life in

the kingdom. This is the fundamental reality of the kingdom.
—*Set Apart: A Six-Week Study of the Beatitudes*, pp. 49–50

On the Cross, His life for mine. In life, His strength for mine. When God gave His Son, He not only gave Him *for us*, He also gave Him *in us*. Have you embraced Him for your salvation? In the same way, lean into Him for your strength.

Marinate Your Heart

Let your heart soak in the truths of Colossians 2:6–7. Mine every word. Ponder every thought. If these words are familiar to you, what are they saying to you afresh? Respond.

So then, just as you received Christ Jesus as LORD, continue to live your lives in him, rooted and built up in him, strengthened in the faith as you were taught, and overflowing with thankfulness. —Colossians 2:6–7

DAY 7

What a relief surrender proves to be. Instead of making you weak, it makes you strong. Carrying all the burdens you were never meant to carry has been weighing you down and holding you back. Now you are full speed ahead. Unencumbered, you are ready for anything.

I love the way God instructed His people to eat the first Passover. They were slaves in Egypt and had been for four generations. So not one living Israelite knew what it meant to be free. Oh, they had heard the stories. They kept the stories alive and dreamed of a day when they would be free again, but not one of them had ever experienced freedom. It was just a concept.

But now the tides were turning. Freedom seemed possible. The how and the when were complete unknowns, but the excitement was spreading. God was on the move. God sent a series of blights on the Egyptians, each more consequential than the one before. Finally, the final scourge would come and God's people were instructed to eat the first Passover. Here is where I want to focus your attention: on the exact way the people were to eat the Passover meal.

> They were to eat the Passover meal quickly, ready to leave at a moment's notice. "This is how you are to eat it: with your cloak tucked into your belt, your sandals on your feet and your staff in your hand. Eat it in haste; it is the LORD's Passover" (Exodus 12:11). When the LORD's command came to

move out, they were not to be hindered by their old lives. They were to be on their feet, packed and dressed for the journey, ready to obey at a moment's notice. They were to be uncluttered—free to leave what lay behind and reach forward to what lay ahead. Free to grab hold of that for which God had grabbed hold of them.

I press on to take hold of that for which Christ Jesus took hold of me. Brothers, I do not consider myself yet to have taken hold of it. But one thing I do: Forgetting what is behind and straining toward what is ahead, I press on toward the goal to win the prize for which God has called me heavenward in Christ Jesus. —Philippians 3:12–14

The call came in the middle of the night. Stop now and read it in Exodus 12: 31–34. Before this, Moses had been demanding that pharaoh let his people go; now pharaoh begged him to take his people out. From one moment to the next, everything can change. Be ready.

The people of God—the great nation—as many as 2 million strong, along with their livestock and the gold and silver they collected from the Egyptians, left Egypt as one. . . . The people who once served the pharaoh's agenda will now be free to serve the LORD.

Notice how the people could have been hindered by their ties to their old life. Even those things they hoped to escape had the potential to keep them bound.

They said to Moses, "Was it because there were no graves in Egypt that you brought us to the desert to die? What have you done to us by bringing us out of Egypt? Didn't we say to you in Egypt, 'Leave us alone; let us serve the Egyptians'? It would have been better for us to serve the Egyptians than to die in the desert!" (Exodus 14:11–12).

> The LORD was determined to set them free. He had provision in place and a plan ready for how to break their attachments to the life they knew so they could embrace something new.
> —*Life Unhindered! Five Keys to Walking in Freedom*, pp. 63–64

Live ready. Pack light. Hold life loosely. God can flip the script at a moment's notice. Surrendered to His plans and His ways, freedom is being worked out in your life from one event to the next. Fully lean into Him. To be on His timetable, surrender is the secret.

Uncluttered

That's what surrender brings into your life—the power to break with the old, tired, restricting ways. The ways that have led you around by the nose for too long. The thought patterns and worries and fears and angers and resentments. As you surrender, those old, useless patterns fall away, little by little. Not in one fell swoop but progressively.

Now when you feel the old baggage start to assert itself and beckon you into emotional chaos, you know what to do. Not fight harder but surrender deeper.

> The power of surrender will take you places in the kingdom you didn't even know existed. More than you can ask or imagine.

Whatever you find yourself picking up, lay it down. You need to be light on your feet. You need to be nimble, agile, deft. You need to be ready for anything.

> Once your flesh is out of the way with its self-centered demands and time-bound outlook, the power of God can begin to flow freely. He can begin to speak to you about what and how to pray. He can give you specific instructions about any actions you should take. —*Live a Praying Life® Workbook (10th Anniversary Edition)*, p. 163

The power of surrender will take you places in the kingdom you didn't even know existed. More than you can ask or imagine.

Marinate Your Heart

Let your heart soak in the truths of Isaiah 43:16–19. Sit with it. Be present with Him as you listen for His voice. What is He saying to you? Respond.

This is what the LORD says—he who made a way through the sea, a path through the mighty waters, who drew out the chariots and horses, the army and reinforcements together, and they lay there, never to rise again, extinguished, snuffed out like a wick: "Forget the former things; do not dwell on the past. See, I am doing a new thing! Now it springs up; do you not perceive it? I am making a way in the wilderness and streams in the wasteland." —Isaiah 43:16–19

EXALT

Glorify the LORD with me; let us exalt his name together.
—Psalm 34:3

DAY 8

Exalt His name. Extol Him. Praise Him. Adore Him. Worship Him. Revel in His presence. Celebrate His works. Here is where you will find joy. In surrender, peace. In praise, joy.

> I will extol the LORD at all times; his praise will always be on my lips. I will glory in the LORD; let the afflicted hear and rejoice. Glorify the LORD with me; let us exalt his name together. —Psalm 34:1–3

Why does God invite and instruct us to praise Him? God loves our praise and worship because He loves us, and our love back to Him delights Him. He is seeking worshippers.

> Yet a time is coming and has now come when the true worshipers will worship the Father in the Spirit and in truth, for they are the kind of worshipers the Father seeks. —John 4:23

Did you catch that? He is *looking for* our worship. Our praise brings Him joy. Think about the expressions of love you delight in most. You love it when the one you most love expresses love to you. The more remote the relationship, the less pleasure you experience. It's nice to be loved by others, but the expressions of love you cherish are from the ones who are closest to you. The fact He loves your praise is further proof He adores you "The prayer of the upright is His delight" (Proverbs 15:8 NASB).

> God loves our praise and worship because He loves us, and our love back to Him delights Him.

When your loved one expresses love to you, how do you respond? Do you remain aloof? Instead, don't you pour out your love right back? As you praise and worship and adore Him, it opens your heart toward Him and the deep love He feels toward you. In exalting Him and adoring Him, you find yourself more aware of His presence. He is not more present—He is always fully present to you—but you are not always fully present to Him. As you deliberately worship Him, the reality of His presence grows. You are more fully present to Him. The wonder of His love for you seeps deep into your heart. You discover what true joy is.

You will make known to me the path of life; in Your presence is fullness of joy; in Your right hand there are pleasures forever. —Psalm 16:11 NASB

Surely you have granted him unending blessings and made him glad with the joy of your presence. —Psalm 21:6

Then I will go to the altar of God, to God, my joy and my delight. I will praise you with the lyre, O God, my God. —Psalm 43:4

In praise, an interchange of love occurs. It may appear as though praise is a one-way street. I praise and worship God. God does not praise and worship me. However, when you look at the real dynamic of praise and how it works, you see it is reciprocal. God does not worship you, but He cherishes you. He treasures you. And that is why He takes such delight in your worship.

The Instigator of Praise

Sometimes praise rises spontaneously. Something happens or we have a thought or some new insight takes hold, and it spurs praise. Other times praise is a deliberate choice. Our inclination is to be self-focused, though we are outgrowing that little by little. Praise takes the focus off ourselves and puts it on Him. It becomes the opposite of self-focused—God focused. I need to deliberately think to praise Him. I need to ask the Holy Spirit to remind me to exalt Him.

When I am reminded by His Spirit to look up and fix my eyes on Him instead of on myself, it is His initiative that calls me. He calls me to praise because He loves me, and He loves my love for Him.

And He knows the power praise releases in your life.

> Child, praise is your best weapon. Something supernaturally powerful happens when you walk in praise. It reorients your thoughts and resets your emotions. I don't remind you to praise Me at all times because I'm a needy, narcissistic God, but because you need it. It strips the enemy of his most potent mechanism—dissatisfaction. It overturns fear and causes faith to sprout. You can't overdo praise. —*Conversations With the Most High: 365 Days in God's Presence*, p. 78

Learn to walk in worship, breathe praise, live a praying life. It is a skill that will serve you well. The Holy Spirit will be your private tutor, patiently schooling you in the art of worship until you are most at home in the atmosphere of praise and thanksgiving.

People who have learned the value of praise and thanksgiving are fortified and ready for whatever life brings. But you learn it in the small things. That's where you integrate it into your life so that it is your default mode. It's like learning a foreign language. You have to practice it and immerse yourself in it until it is so much a part of you that you even think in your new vocabulary of praise. —*The Power of Small: Think Small to Live Large*, p. 90

Marinate Your Heart

Practice praise and worship right now. On purpose. Let the eyes of your heart see the reality of His presence with you. You are not imagining. Rather you are using your visually oriented brain to focus on what is entirely real. Scripture promises He is fully present to you. Let your heart soak in this truth, thought by thought, word by word.

On that day you will realize that I am in my Father, and *you are in me*, and *I am in you*. Whoever has my commands and keeps them is the one who loves me. The one who loves me will be loved by my Father, and I too will love them and *show myself to them*. . . . Anyone who loves me will obey my teaching. My Father will love them, and *we will come to them and make our home* with them. —John 14:20–21, 23, emphasis added

And surely *I am with you always*, to the very end of the age. —Matthew 28:20, emphasis added

DAY 9

His love for you is the inflow that produces an outflow called praise and worship. Praise is always a response. His love for you is the catalyst for everything that happens in the spiritual arena, from your salvation to

> His love for you is the inflow that produces an outflow called praise and worship.

every inch of spiritual growth, to every nuance of understanding the truth, to every prayer you pray, to every moment of worship. All Him and His tender, passionate love for you.

> Child, the absolute certainty of My love is the glue that holds everything together. It is the one thing that makes sense of life, and the reality that defines all other reality. The promise of My unfailing love anchors the heart, no matter what. Here is a promise that can burrow into the depths of your heart and make a home there: I will never forget you, abandon you, or fail you. You are so precious to Me that you are never out of My thoughts; you are never left out in the cold.
> —*Conversations With the Most High: 365 Days in God's Presence*, p. 80

As you ponder His love for you, let the depth of it take hold. He doesn't simply love you in some sterile, generic kind of way. You are not one of a herd. He loves *you*. You!

Child, here in My presence, no words are necessary. Here you are safe, and loved, and fully known. I understand things about you that you don't understand about yourself, and love you completely—not *in spite of those* things, but *in* those things. I don't have to overlook anything about you in order to cherish you with all My heart. You are Mine.
—*Conversations With the Most High: 365 Days in God's Presence*, p. 22

We imagine He sees first our failures and our shame. That's what we see. We see all the reasons we do not deserve to be loved, and our enemy encourages such thoughts. See how clever that ploy is? If you think God is forever disappointed in you, or angry at you, or ready to scold you, then His presence is not appealing. Do you have anyone in your life who is critical and always correcting you? Do you love that person's presence?

Worship is being fully abandoned to His presence, fully trusting that His love for you is unshakeable. If you have been trained to feel fearful and humiliated in His presence, then the call to worship Him is less appealing. Does He convict us of our sins? Of course. We'll talk about that in the next section. But even that comes from love. And He doesn't greet your praise with a performance review.

Maybe you have been taught that it is a mark of humility to feel shamefaced in the presence of God. Let me ask you this: Is it humility to replace God's truth with your own version of reality? Or is that arrogance? If that thought hit home, now you're ashamed of your shame. Stop. Release all shame and regret. Hand it over to Him. He is not bringing this to your attention to beat you down. He is showing you a new way to think so you will be free and abandoned in His presence.

As I write these words, I have a crop of little grandchildren. The oldest is six and they go down to three weeks. Little. They haven't learned yet to be restrained in their expressions of joy or delight. They take ridiculous joy in my presence. When I drive into the driveway, they run to meet me. They jump up and down. They squeal and scream. They jump into my arms. They want to tell me everything they have been doing and show me everything about their lives. They want me to share in all their pleasures and accomplishments.

And the ridiculous joy is mutual. Their joy in my presence brings me such delight. I can't get enough of them. There are times when we talk or play that I take the opportunity to give some guidance or suggest some course corrections, but that does not diminish my absolute jubilation in being with them. That's not what I think of when I think of them. I just love them enough to occasionally add a suggestion or two.

God loves us enough to make the corrections that will guide us to our best life. But our flaws and weaknesses and failures are not how He defines us.

It is because of him that you are in Christ Jesus, who has become for us wisdom from God—that is, our righteousness, holiness and redemption. —1 Corinthians 1:30

God made him who had no sin to be sin for us, so that in him we might become the righteousness of God. —2 Corinthians 5:21

Unbridled Joy

When we get hold of the reality of God's ridiculous love for us and His unbridled joy in our presence, then praise and worship come naturally. You won't be able to hold it in. If you were to challenge me to remain stoic and distant when my grandchildren greet me, I wouldn't take the challenge. I couldn't do it. Nor would I want to. It would be unnatural and stifling.

Respond to His love and joy. That's what praise and worship are. Let His love ignite your love. Let His delight be the force that sparks your delight. Abandon yourself to Him.

Marinate Your Heart

Let the truths of the following Scripture passages put down deep roots. Let the Holy Spirit guide your thoughts through every word and phrase. Respond.

Steadfast love surrounds the one who trusts in the LORD.
—Psalm 32:10 ESV

I will sing of the steadfast love of the LORD, forever; with my mouth I will make known your faithfulness to all generations.
—Psalm 89:1 ESV

See what kind of *love the Father has given to us*, that we should be called children of God. —1 John 3:1 ESV, emphasis added

DAY 10

God loves praise because He loves you. But God does not *need* praise. You need to praise. Praise benefits you.

Let's think about how praise enhances your life. First, praise sets your focus correctly.

> We were built to be God-focused. That's the condition under which we thrive. . . . Self-consciousness is not our natural state. No one except God is worthy of such concentrated attention. The proper focus of all aspects of our personality is to put God first (Matthew 6:33). . . . We were not fashioned to be self-focused. It doesn't work. We break down under it. Why? Because we are not worthy of worship. The world was not created to revolve around you. You can't handle it; it's not your role. We were made to be worshippers. —*Altar'd: Experience the Power of Resurrection*, p. 90

Praise focuses our thoughts in the right place. When we are caught up in our own limited scope and our emotions are dictated by our own skewed perceptions, our lives are off-kilter. We are letting a lie or an optical illusion act as the basis for our evaluation of our circumstances. Faith is how we are to navigate our lives. When we try, as Paul says, to walk by sight, we don't have the whole picture. Praise and worship opens our hearts to God's point of view and lifts our eyes from the situation and puts them on Him.

> What we can observe from earth is only the appearance; it is not the truth. Faith acts in harmony with truth and disregards appearance. The circumstances of earth are like an optical illusion. When you look at an optical illusion, your eyes tell you one thing, but the truth is something else. You can only interpret an optical illusion correctly if you understand the principles of how the background affects the foreground. You have to *know* something that you do not see. Otherwise, you will believe a lie. —*Live a Praying Life® Workbook (10th Anniversary Edition),* p. 86

When our focus is on the Supply rather than the need, everything looks different. Our vantage point gives us a new view.

> Keep your focus on the Supplier, not the need. Whatever is in the foreground of your thoughts will loom largest. If your difficulty or need takes up the most real estate of your thought life, then it will loom largest. Train your brain to divert thoughts of the need to thoughts of the Supplier. Live a God-focused life of praise. "So we fix our eyes not on what is seen, but on what is unseen, since what is seen is temporary, but what is unseen is eternal" (2 Corinthians 4:18). —*Prayer Fatigue*: *Ten Ways to Revive Your Prayer Life*, p. 122

Viewpoint is everything. From the window of an airplane in flight, the earth's tallest mountain looks miniature. From the foot of that mountain, it appears massive and intimidating. From our own earthly view, the circumstances of our lives can appear hopeless and overwhelming. But with God in view, the scale changes and what looked too big is shown to be under control.

God is the big picture. When He is the focal point, then everything else takes on the proper dimensions. We see things in
perspective. Big God. Little circumstances. . . . Refocus. Get
God in view. Let yourself be strengthened and enabled.
Receive. When we are God-focused, we can stand firm. We
won't be pushed and shoved by circumstances. We can live
lives of courage and integrity. We can let our lives flow in
service to others. We don't have to be diminished by events.
—*Life Unhindered! Five Keys to Walking in Freedom*, p. 46

Faith's View

Praise and worship flips a switch in our hearts so we are redirected
in our thoughts and emotions. It is impossible to give yourself
to praise and remain caught up in yourself. God Himself, by His
Holy Spirit, is active in your praise and worship. He reminds you
of Who He is, how worthy of praise He is, how able He is to work
out everything for your benefit, and how precious you are to Him.
Praise is more than you saying nice things about God. Praise is a
gift God pours out on you because praise has the power to redirect
your gaze from you to Him, from problem to answer.

> Fix your eyes on Jesus. Lock your gaze on Him. Everything
> else can be perceived correctly if His presence is the reference
> point.
>   Your mind always needs a reference point to correctly
> see reality. For example, imagine that you see a photograph
> of an object and the object fills the frame. It looks big. Then
> you see a photograph of that same object, but held in a per-
> son's hand. Now, with the hand as a reference point, your
> perception of the object's size changes.

Or, imagine that you are in a traffic jam and all around you are big trucks that obscure your view of the horizon. If the trucks begin to move, it will feel as though you are the one moving. When your horizon comes back in view, you will reorient and know that you are sitting still. The horizon is your reference point. Without a reference point, your perceptions are skewed. Jesus invites us to make His presence our one and only reference point, the basis for our orientation. Fix your eyes on Him.

Do an experiment with me. Look around and find a single object to fasten your eyes on. Pick something about an arm's length away. Now stare fixedly at it for several seconds. What happens to your view of surrounding objects when your eyes are locked on a single object? Everything else is a little bit blurred and out of focus. That object on which you have fixed your attention is clear and focused. When we get our eyes locked on Jesus, His presence is our reality. Nothing else seems so compelling or so worthy of attention. His face fills our frame of reference and everything else pales. —*Life Unhindered! Five Keys to Walking in Freedom*, pp. 143–144

Marinate Your Heart

Let your heart soak in the truths of the following Scripture passages. Take it in and taste every morsel. Word by word, phrase by phrase, thought by thought. Respond.

My eyes are ever on the LORD, for only he will release my feet from the snare. —Psalm 25:15

I lift up my eyes to you, to you who sit enthroned in heaven.
As the eyes of slaves look to the hand of their master, as the
eyes of a female slave look to the hand of her mistress, so our
eyes look to the LORD our God, till he shows us his mercy.
—Psalm 123:1–2

Fixing our eyes on Jesus, the pioneer and perfecter of faith.
  —Hebrews 12:2

DAY 11

Praise has power. I love to explain things, but I can't explain the power of praise. Though I can't explain it, I know it. I experience it. When we deliberately,

> Praise has power.

purposefully praise God, some kind of transaction takes place in the spiritual realm and the atmosphere of your heart changes. It is sometimes a discipline we choose.

> Let anxiety and worry be a trigger to turn to praise. Praise is what brings God and His greatness to center stage in our minds. When worry starts whispering, begin to praise God. Make praise your habit all the time. . . .
>
> Don't give voice to fear. I don't mean don't talk about your troubling circumstances. But I am saying skip the fearful commentary: "Things will never change. It's too late now. Things only go from bad to worse." When you say such things, it just reinforces fear in your mind. You are lining up with the lie. Instead, say the truth, even when you don't feel like you believe it at the moment. "God is in control. God is working out everything toward His good resolution. God loves and cherishes me."
>
> You'll find your own ways to be disciplined about keeping your focus right. Just do it. Don't allow your circumstances to distract you from the provision God has put in place. Shift your focus from yourself to God. —*Life Unhindered! Five Keys to Walking in Freedom*, p. 99

Exchange a habit of worry for a habit of praise. Train yourself until an old habit has been routed and a new habit takes its place. In consciously deciding to praise instead of worry, be specific in your praise. Notice how the psalmist frames his expressions of worship:

> Praise the LORD, my soul; all my inmost being, praise his holy name. Praise the LORD, my soul, and forget not all his benefits—who forgives all your sins and heals all your diseases, who redeems your life from the pit and crowns you with love and compassion, who satisfies your desires with good things so that your youth is renewed like the eagle's. —Psalm 103:1–5

"Forget not all his benefits." Don't forget all the benefits—add-ons. He saved you and secured your eternal destiny by sending His own Son to pay the penalty you owed. And beyond *that*, added to *that*, on top of *that*—He has done *immeasurably more.*

> Now to him who is able to do immeasurably more than all we ask or imagine, according to his power that is at work within us. —Ephesians 3:20

As a praise booster, list His benefits. Recall His work in your life. Look for His kindnesses.

> I had learned the power of thanksgiving through the course of many circumstances, but the death of my husband made all the others seem miniscule. The LORD reminded me daily, and reminds me daily still, that He holds my husband, my sons, and me in His hands and that He is working out everything towards an end that is good, pleasing, and perfect.

Let me share with you some of my journal entries from the darkest hours.

When negative, self-pitying, fearful thoughts knock on the door of my mind and seek admittance, I have a plan. I can't wish them away, or stick my fingers in my ears, or deny that they are there. That won't work. Instead, I will use a spiritual chemotherapy against them. I will target them for destruction by directing the power of praise right at the core of them. I have formulated an aggressive, overpowering spiritual cocktail of truth, praise, peace, and thanksgiving. . . .

I am crowned with tender mercies . . . such as:

For 26 years I have had a life partner who encourages me to follow my vision, and who rejoices with me in my successes and spurs me on in my disappointments. I have never had to hold myself back or deny my abilities in order to protect a fragile ego. Because of Wayne, I could be fully me.

We have three grown sons whose character is formed and solid. We are comforted to know that they are strong and that their faith is real.

We see daily the provision made for us before we knew that we would need it. For example, our middle son, Kennedy, a recent Baylor graduate, had planned several months ago to move home for a while and save on expenses while he pursues some opportunities. He arrived home on the night before we received Wayne's diagnosis. We have Kennedy at home to help us just when we need him.

We have a lifetime collection of friends to stand beside us.

We have extended families who give us strength and support.

I have a career that leaves me in charge of my own schedule.

I had an office away from home for 15 years, but after our youngest left for college, I moved my office home. How much easier that makes these coming days!

*I have an assistant, Terry Trieu, who is the most compe-
tent and responsible person on earth and whom I can count
on completely. She knows how to run my daily business better
than I do!*

*We are, indeed, crowned with tender mercies, of which
this list is but a shadow.*
—*Heart's Cry: Principles of Prayer*, pp. 79–81

In calling us to live a life of praise, God is not calling us to simply
live by emotion. The truth about Him and His ways provides ample
foundation for exalting Him. Praise is based on reality; worry or
discouragement is based on emotion. Emotion will catch up with
reality when we stay stubbornly moored in the truth. "We have this
hope as an anchor for the soul, firm and secure" (Hebrews 6:19).
No matter what your eyes see, your heart knows a higher reality.
Focus there.

Marinate Your Heart

Soak in the truths of Psalm 9:1–2. Let them burrow into your heart.
Receive them—every word, every phrases, every thought. Respond.

I will give thanks to you, LORD, with all my heart; I will tell
of all your wonderful deeds. I will be glad and rejoice in
you; I will sing the praises of your name, O Most High.
—Psalm 9:1–2

DAY 12

Praise and thanksgiving are two parts of a whole. It is commonly said that praise is about who He is and thanksgiving is about what He does. How do we know who His is? We know by what He does. What He does tells us who He is. That is why He tells His story. That is why Scripture is a record of His activity among His people. His Word does not speak abstractly but concretely. In the story of His work in the lives of others we see who God is.

> His actions throw light on His name. What He does demonstrates and authenticates His name. His actions are an exact reflection of His nature. What He does is proof of who He is. . . . The word *integrity* means a state of wholeness or completeness or unity. God has perfect integrity. His actions are perfectly consistent with His character. —*Power in the Name of Jesus*, p. 16

Each time God reveals His name in the Old Testament, He first shows what that name means. The revelation of an aspect of His Great Name is preceded by a demonstration of His great power. Show and tell.

For example, He reveals His name as *El Roi*—the God Who Sees—as He pursues the rejected and outcast Hagar, betrayed by those she trusted and thrust into the wilderness alone and vulnerable. She discovers God pursued her and knew her and saw her where she is (Genesis 16:1–13).

Or when He revealed His name *El Shaddai*—God Almighty—He revealed it to Abram (later Abraham) and Sarai (later Sarah) as He made an outrageous promise to them. He promised the barren and aged couple, long past childbearing years, that a son would be born to them within a year. Only an Almighty God could bring about such an impossible end. And God Almighty produced what He promised (Genesis 17:1–22).

Show and tell. In the Book of John, Jesus makes seven I Am claims, and as He does, He continues the same pattern. What He does proves who He is.

For example, before He proclaims Himself the Bread of Life, He first feeds the crowd of more than five thousand with a few loaves and fishes. He fills their hunger and satisfies their needs by providing more than enough out of not enough. Then He moves them to the deeper truth His physical miracle pointed to.

> Jesus used this opening to begin to point their hearts toward kingdom realities. Jesus' reply to them is often interpreted as if it were a rebuke, but I'm not sure that's the case here. Jesus knew human nature. "He did not need man's testimony about man, for he knew what was in a man" (John 2:25). He knew that they would be attracted to Him by His miracles. That's one reason He performed miracles. John calls His miracles "signs." A sign points to something. Jesus was going to explain to them what the sign pointed to, and that had been His desire all along.
>
> I think that Jesus' reply sounded more like this. I think when He answered them, His eyes had a sparkle and a smile lit His face. "You have followed Me all this way. You have gone to all the trouble to find out where I went. Then you did whatever you had to do to get here. You have worked hard to find Me. And for what? I don't think it was really the

miracle I performed. It was what the miracle did for you. You ate the loaves and were filled and satisfied. You have worked hard to find me because I gave You something that satisfied your hunger."

The crowd is hanging on His every word. They are shaking their heads and nodding assent to one another. "Yes. That's right. That's exactly it. Your miracle provided what I needed." Otherwise, you see, it would just have been a magic show. So that's the response Jesus wanted. He wanted them to seek Him out for what He could do for them.

Then, His voice animated, He continues, "If you liked that, you won't believe what I really have for you! That's nothing compared to what I can really give you."

The crowd is electrified. Their curiosity about how He got there is forgotten. They know the words He is about to speak will matter to their lives. They lean forward to catch every word. "You worked that hard for food that spoils. Listen! Don't work for food that spoils—temporary, transient stuff. I fed you yesterday until you could eat no more, and today you're hungry again. Work that hard for food that endures—stays with you. Food that will give you eternal life. Sure, I can feed you bread for you bodies. But I can do more than that. I can give you eternal life." —*Power in the Name of Jesus*, p. 35

What He does is not divorced from Who He is. One is not complete without the other.

"I will remember the deeds of the LORD; yes, I will remember your miracles of long ago. I will consider all your works and meditate on all your mighty deeds." Your ways, God, are holy. What god is as great as our God? You are the God who performs miracles; you display your power among the peoples. —Psalm 77:11–14

Remember

An aid in remembering the LORD's work in your life and in the lives of those around you is to record it. Journal it. When I am at my most discouraged, I thumb through my old journals. They remind me of times when I thought all was lost and my situation would never change. Times when I was down and discouraged. Now I can see the result. I've let the whole situation unfold to its conclusion and the narrative has changed. I can identify all the places God worked when I thought He was silent.

Consider starting a journal. Keep track of what you are experiencing in the moment and know this present moment will soon be part of your past. From that perspective you will redefine your right now.

Another option is to keep a gratitude journal. Write down everything you are grateful for even in the smallest details of life. Let it be a family project. You will be surprised at how this active praise project will train you to "set your heart on things above" (Colossians 3:1).

Tell someone else. I think the best place for this is in a small prayer group. One thing I love about my long-term prayer partners is we know each other's history, and we can say, "Remember that time?" And we all know what the other is talking about.

Marinate Your Heart

Let the words of Scripture put down roots. Take time with these words. Respond.

You, God, are my God, earnestly I seek you; I thirst for you,
my whole being longs for you, in a dry and parched land
where there is no water. I have seen you in the sanctuary and
beheld your power and your glory. Because your love is better
than life, my lips will glorify you. I will praise you as long as
I live, and in your name I will lift up my hands. I will be fully
satisfied as with the richest of foods; with singing lips my
mouth will praise you. On my bed I remember you; I think
of you through the watches of the night. Because you are my
help, I sing in the shadow of your wings. I cling to you; your
right hand upholds me. —Psalm 63:1–8

DAY 13

> Always giving thanks to God the Father for everything, in the name of our Lᴏʀᴅ Jesus Christ. —Ephesians 5:20
>
> Give thanks in all circumstances; for this is God's will for you in Christ Jesus. —1 Thessalonians 5:18
>
> Do not be anxious about anything, but in every situation, by prayer and petition, with thanksgiving, present your requests to God —Philippians 4:6

In these passages, do you see the words *always*, *everything*, *all, anything, every*? The call to praise and thanksgiving is all-inclusive. No exceptions. Why? For our sake. We need it. Living in a grateful state of mind and heart ushers us into the life God intends. He has designed a life of joy and peace and steadiness. Out of His great love for us and His desire to see us experience the full measure of His plan for our good, He invites us to live in praise and gratitude.

> Out of His great love for us and His desire to see us experience the full measure of His plan for our good, He invites us to live in praise and gratitude.

Our flesh (human nature) presents a few stumbling blocks to living in praise—going beyond saying "thank You" to being thankful, full of thanks as our natural state. Let's tackle some of those obstacles.

> "Every good and perfect gift is from above, coming down from the Father of the heavenly lights, who does not change like shifting shadows" (James 1:17). It seems obvious to thank God for the good things He brings to life. This is the most elementary lesson in the school of prayer. Yet, we don't do it very well. Two stumbling blocks occasionally enter my life and dilute my spontaneous, continuous giving of thanks for God's good gifts.
>
> First, I delight in the gift and exclude the Giver. Of course, I'm well trained and would rarely neglect to say thank you to God at some point. But my delight is in the gift. I forget that God's supply is meant to point me to Him, the Source. He delivers because He is the Deliverer. He blesses because He is the Blesser. He provides because He is the Provider. He rescues because He is the Rescuer. He is revealed in everything He does. His good things and perfect gifts are signposts pointing to Him. "I have loved you with an everlasting love; I have drawn you with loving-kindness" (Jeremiah 31:3).
>
> When I allow God's goodness to point me to Him, I take nothing for granted. Everything in my life is a reason for thanksgiving. . . .
>
> Everything points me to God, the source of every good gift. By building in me a thankful heart, He sensitizes me to His constant presence. By training yourself to acknowledge the good things that are so freely and so reliably given to you, you are keeping Him in view. When I fill my days with praise and thanksgiving, the problems and crises that come along are dwarfed by my awareness of His loving-kindness.

The second barrier to a thankful heart is that sometimes I look at my life from a one-dimensional perspective, and I see hurdles and disappointments galore. . . . Soon, all the good and perfect gifts with which my life is filled are lost in the jumble of dissatisfactions. . . .

When I am in this thankless state of mind, my whole life, especially my prayer life, is out of sync. My spirit is clothed in garments that don't fit. I am to be wearing "a garment of praise instead of a spirit of despair" (Isaiah 61:3). My outward expression does not reflect the Holy Spirit's work within me. . . .

Praise and thanksgiving do not magically change my circumstances. They radically alter my viewpoint. Praise and thanksgiving bring me back into the presence of God, where there is fullness of joy and pleasures evermore. —*Heart's Cry: Principles of Prayer*, pp. 74–76

Marinate Your Heart

Soak in the truths of Psalm 100:1–5. Steep your heart and mind in them. Respond.

Shout for joy to the LORD, all the earth. Worship the LORD with gladness; come before him with joyful songs. Know that the LORD is God. It is he who made us, and we are his; we are his people, the sheep of his pasture. Enter his gates with thanksgiving and his courts with praise; give thanks to him and praise his name. For the LORD is good and his love endures forever; his faithfulness continues through all generations. —Psalm 100:1–5

DAY 14

Praise and thanksgiving will inoculate you against discouragement and fear and hopelessness and anger and the many other emotions that will sabotage your life. Preemptive praise and thanksgiving is the key to walking in victory. You can thank God and praise Him before you see what He is going to do, before you recognize what He is doing. You can praise Him because you know what you know.

> Praise and thanksgiving will inoculate you against discouragement and fear and hopelessness and anger and the many other emotions that will sabotage your life.

The joy that flows from Jesus into your heart is outside of and beyond circumstances. It is a joy that surpasses the happiness that earthly success brings. True joy is so Christ-centered that earthly success can neither add to it nor diminish it. . . .

God wants you to take great pleasure in what He provides and to find joy in it because you know it came from Him.

However, there will be other times when His blessings and His favor do not come in material, financial, or physical form. There will be times when from the point of view of earth it will appear that God is withholding His blessing. There will be times when your circumstances seem not to be the platform for God's power. Then what? "Though the fig tree does not bud and there are no grapes on the vines, though the olive crop fails and the fields produce no food, though there are no sheep in the pen and no cattle in the stalls, yet I will rejoice in the Lord, I will be joyful in God my Savior" (Habakkuk 3:16–18). Joy, when it is truly joy, will not abandon you even then.

Under the surface of your emotions you will discover a strong undercurrent of joy. It is His joy. It is eternal; it is changeless; it is His gift to you. It is yours when you live in an altar'd state.

You can rejoice because you know that God is in control. You can rejoice because you know that God is working everything out for His good purposes. You can rejoice in advance for what God will do. You can rejoice because you know that nothing is too difficult for Him and nothing is impossible to Him. You can rejoice because He is doing something that is beyond what you can ask or even imagine. You can rejoice *in the Lord*. . . .

Joy expresses itself in praise. Praise is the spontaneous and natural outflow of the inflow of His Life. . . .

Praise completes the experience of joy. The more my soul is filled with Him, the more of His joy that floods me, the more "my mouth is filled with [His] praise" (Psalm 71:8) and "my lips overflow with praise" (Psalm 119:171). . . . The soul can only be satisfied with the presence of God through the indwelling life of Christ because that is its destiny. Because God has "set eternity in the hearts of men" (Ecclesiastes 3:11), nothing less than eternity—nothing temporal—will satisfy. . . .

Not only will praise complete the experience of joy, but it will also multiply the joy. In the times when your emotions are at their lowest and when the joy of the Lord seems faint, begin to offer praise. . . . Your decision to offer praise will give the Spirit ascendancy over your flesh. Praise is one of the most powerful weapons in your war against flesh life. —*Altar'd: Experience the Power of Resurrection*, pp. 177–179

The Weapon of Praise

Praise is a potent weapon. As you praise, you release tremendous spiritual power. Praise dispels the enemy's troops. Praise lays the groundwork for the display of God's power. Psalm 50:23 says, "Those who sacrifice thank offerings honor me, and to the blameless I will show my salvation."

The praises of His people have God's life in them. In the spiritual realm, we are always the responders and the receivers, and God is always the initiator and the giver. This is even so in praise. It is the Spirit of the Son in us who is stirring up praise, who is bringing to our thoughts all the reasons God is worthy of our praise, who is expressing His joy through our praise. When I praise God, it is really the Son praising through me. I am speaking the words of praise that He is speaking in me. His words coming through my mouth have the life of God in them because His words are life. The praises of God's people have God's life in them; He inhabits the praises of His people.

Marinate Your Heart

Absorb the truths of Psalm 33:20–22, and let them find a home in you. Let these words—words that are life—take up residence in your heart. Respond.

We wait in hope for the LORD; he is our help and our shield. In him our hearts rejoice, for we trust in his holy name. May your unfailing love be with us, LORD, even as we put our hope in you. —Psalm 33:20–22

EXPOSE

Search me, God, and know my heart; test me and know my anxious thoughts. See if there is any offensive way in me, and lead me in the way everlasting. —Psalm 139:23–24

DAY 15

Confession, repentance, and cleansing are essential in a praying life. If prayer is the conduit through which God's power and provision flow into the circumstances of earth, then surely we need to keep that conduit uncluttered so power can flow more freely. As we begin to think about exposing our hearts to God for His conviction, correction, and cleansing, let's first recognize that it is, once more, His love for us that draws us to a realization of sin in our lives. You don't have to think of this as excruciating. As you commit to opening your heart to His convicting, anticipate experiencing yet another dimension of His love for you that refuses to leave you saddled with the burden of sin in your life and is instead determined to see you free.

He will not shame, belittle, degrade, or scold you. He will cleanse you and relieve you and bring you further into the bounty He has available to you. He wants to remove the elements in your life that diminish you and restrict you and hold you hostage. Is there an aspect of sorrow associated with being confronted with sin? Of course. Sin does not fit you. Recognizing and admitting sin brings godly sorrow. But it also brings joy. As if you have been weighted down and now the weight has been removed and you discover new energy, new motivation, new vitality. "Let us also lay aside every weight, and sin which clings so closely, and let us run with endurance the race that is set before us" (Hebrews 12:1 ESV).

> Child, I hate sin because I love you. Sin diminishes you and
> hinders you and wounds you. My warning away from sin is
> from a bottomless well of passionate love. To see how much
> I hate sin, you need only look at the Cross. To see how much
> I love you, you need only look at the Cross. "By the cross
> we know the gravity of sin and the greatness of God's love
> toward us" (John Chrysostom). —*Conversations with the
> Most High: 365 Days in God's Presence*, p. 71

Blinded by Sin

Sin blinds us to the true nature of our Father. Besmirched by sin,
we feel ashamed and unworthy, and so we hide from and run from
the One who longs to fold us into His arms and greet us with a kiss.
See how Jesus described a father's response to his wandering son:
"But while he was still a long way off, his father saw him and was
filled with compassion for him; he ran to his son, threw his arms
around him and kissed him" (Luke 15:20). When we respond to
His loving conviction, His joy is boundless. No holding it against
us. No making us earn our way back into His good graces.

Let's get a clear view of how God deals with our sins, once we
have turned to Him for salvation.

> Jesus has earned God's goodness for us. From the moment
> we receive Him as our personal Savior, we are becoming on
> the outside—in the reality of daily living—what we have
> been made on the inside.
>
> It is a progression that starts at our new birth and goes on
> until our physical death, but it is always moving forward. Some-
> times the progress is accelerated, and other times it moves so
> slowly it seems to be stalled. But righteousness is always gaining
> ground. We are always, as Athanasius of Alexandria stated,
> "becoming by grace what God is by nature" (*De Incarnatione*, I).

In a praying life, God is using every situation, every moment in our lives, to move us forward in righteousness. His goal is not that we get to the place where we deserve His goodness because that will never happen. His goal is that we progress in the righteousness for which we were designed. At the moment of our salvation, Jesus came to live in us and from that point forward is doing the work only He can do. First, He has made you worthy in God's eyes by paying in full for your every sin and assigning His own righteousness to you as if it were yours. Second, He undertakes to do in you the work that you cannot accomplish on your own. Because of Jesus, you stand before God unashamed and worthy. . . . In his letter to the Romans, Paul says this: "He who did not spare his own Son, but gave him up for us all—how will he not also, along with him, graciously give us all things?" (Romans 8:32). You are worth everything to God. He did not hold back even His most cherished, most prized, most adored Son Jesus to win you and bring you into relationship with Him. Do you really think now that He is standing back and criticizing you and devaluing you? You are utterly precious to Him, warts and all. Prayer is what He has established to keep you close to His heart, not to put you under His microscope and look for flaws.

The Scripture tells us that we are clothed with Christ. "Rather, clothe yourselves with the LORD Jesus Christ, and do not think about how to gratify the desires of the flesh" (Romans 13:14). "All of you who were baptized into Christ have clothed yourselves with Christ" (Galatians 3:27).

Not only does Jesus fill you on the inside, but He covers you on the outside. The reason we can stand unashamed in God's presence is because we are clothed in Christ. Contrast that with our condition apart from Christ. No matter how many good deeds we perform, "all our righteous acts are like filthy rags" (Isaiah 64:6). Our old past attempts to be good enough, which ended in failure, are replaced by the very presence of Christ in our lives. We are washed clean, made spotless, and robed in the righteousness of Jesus. You have been made deserving. —*Prayer Fatigue: Ten Ways to Revive Your Prayer Life*, pp. 67–69

His dealings with us in conviction and drawing us to repentance are part of that strategy. He is relieving us of the sins that distort our view of His love. Get your perspective straight. God convicts of sins because He loves us and wants us to live in joy and freedom.

Marinate Your Heart

Let the Holy Spirit speak the truth of Psalm 51:7–9 deep into your heart. Hear the tenderness of His love for you. Respond.

Cleanse me with hyssop, and I will be clean; wash me, and I will be whiter than snow. Let me hear joy and gladness; let the bones you have crushed rejoice. Hide your face from my sins and blot out all my iniquity. —Psalm 51:7–9

DAY 16

As we expose our hearts to the Spirit's conviction and correction, not only does He forgive our confessed sin, but He also works to cleanse us of its source. The sins we commit are the result of the unrighteousness lurking in us. Sinful behaviors—actions, thoughts, attitudes—are but the symptom of an underlying infection that needs to be healed and cleansed. We are not left to fight in our own power against sins that seem to trip us up time and again. Confession is not just about repentance. It is about cleansing.

> The life of Jesus, Jesus Himself, flows through me. . . . The Scripture tells us that when we confess our sins, two things happen: (1) He forgives us our sins, and (2) He purifies us from all unrighteousness. That fountain, Zechariah said, is for cleansing from both sin (the sinful actions we engage in) and impurity (the unrighteousness that causes us to sin). [See Zechariah 13:1.] In Isaiah 53:5 we read, "He was pierced for our transgressions, he was crushed for our iniquities." The word for "transgressions" (*pesha*) means "rebellion or revolt"—the attitude that produces the act; the word for "iniquities" (*avon*) means "mischief, behavior, fault"—the actions of sin we commit. He died for both our rebellious attitude and the sins that it produces. —*Power in the Blood of Christ*, p. 37

He has designed for us a full spectrum salvation that takes into account the whole picture—the sins we commit and the unrighteousness that causes us to commit them.

> "If we confess our sins, he is faithful and just and will forgive us our sins and purify us from all unrighteousness" (1 John 1:9). When we come into agreement with Him about our helpless and wretched condition, He does two things. He (1) forgives our sins; and He (2) purifies us of all unrighteousness.
>
> Our problem is twofold, and His provision takes care of both. We have the problem of the sins we commit—the behaviors we engage in for which we are culpable and which create a separation from God. Sins that have to be atoned for. We also have the problem of the unrighteousness that causes us to commit sins. Sin and sins.
>
> His plan for securing our salvation was not half-baked. His plan takes into account the whole problem. Suppose that Jesus took care of our sins by atoning for them Himself, but then left us in the condition that had caused the problem in the first place. He would have left us to live in defeat and failure and hopelessness. But the amazing plan for our redemption includes a remedy both for our sins and for our sin. . . .
>
> Our full spectrum salvation includes what Christ did for us, and who Christ is in us. . . .
>
> Because of His life in us, we can experience His life through us. . . .
>
> He has worked out a salvation that takes care of the root of unrighteousness that grows a fruit called sin. . . . Our salvation has two components: (1) what Christ did for us, and (2) who Christ is in us. We have a twofold solution for a twofold problem. Jesus poured out His life for us so He

> could pour out His life in us. —*Altar'd: Experience the Power of Resurrection*, pp. 85–86

The life He lives in you, He wants to live through you. He is ready, and He is able to live His victorious life with you as the epicenter. "Now to him who is able to do immeasurably more than all we ask or imagine, according to *his power* that is at work *within us*" (Ephesians 3:20).

Whiter Than Snow

His plan for repentance makes us clean both inside and out. Our sins are immediately forgiven and not held against us. "If you, LORD, kept a record of sins, LORD, who could stand? But with you there is forgiveness, so that we can, with reverence, serve you" (Psalm 130:3–4). The unrighteousness that produced those sins is being cleansed as He lives and works in us at the deepest parts of our being. "Cleanse me with hyssop, and I will be clean; wash me, and I will be whiter than snow" (Psalm 51:7). Hyssop was an herb used symbolically for cleansing, but in everyday life it was used in foods. So hyssop was taken internally to cleanse on the inside. Cleanse me with hyssop—make me clean inside. Wash me—make me clean on the outside.

God's love is calling you to repentance. He is revealing to you the areas of your life that need to be revealed and exposed so you can offer them to Him for His cleansing work.

Marinate Your Heart

Read Psalm 103:10–14 slowly and deliberately. Think about these verses. Mine their depths. Respond.

> He does not treat us as our sins deserve or repay us according to our iniquities. For as high as the heavens are above the earth, so great is his love for those who fear him; as far as the east is from the west, so far has he removed our transgressions from us. As a father has compassion on his children, so the LORD has compassion on those who fear him; for he knows how we are formed, he remembers that we are dust. —Psalm 103:10–14

DAY 17

Cleansed, inside and out. Washed clean. Purified. Absolved. Do those words fall appealingly on your ear? Do you embrace them? This is what repentance is about. Not punishment. Jesus took care of that. We read, "God demonstrates his own love for us in this: While we were still sinners, Christ died for us" (Romans 5:8). Not shame. Romans 8:1 reminds us there is no condemnation for us: "Therefore, there is now no condemnation for those who are in Christ Jesus."

As you invite God to search your heart, you are not asking Him to bludgeon you with guilt. You are asking Him to reveal those things that are holding you back and to wash them away. His heart-searching love relentlessly pinpoints the places where sin is diluting your strength, lessening your power.

My friend Anne Salorio writes the following:

> Psalm 51 has a lot of references to cleanliness. "Create in me a *clean* heart." "Blot out my transgressions. Wash away all my iniquity and cleanse me from my sin."
>
> A lot of people, understandably, cringe at these cleanliness metaphors. No one wants to be seen as dirty. Dirty is less valuable, undesirable, unwanted. But let's reexamine some other words: *dirty* and *clean.* In my experience, we don't clean things because there's anything truly wrong with dirt, dust, or whatever else. Dirt is perfectly natural. It's part of the world. There are places where we inevitably find it. But the problem is that it obscures the beauty of the thing

beneath it. *We don't clean things as a way to punish the object for being dirty. We clean them because the natural state has been obscured.* Outside of specific circumstances, getting a little dirty doesn't fundamentally devalue an object. It's simply an inevitability that can be confronted as it occurs.

Obviously, this is not a perfect metaphor. . . . Our sins are typically caused by our own choices, not just the passage of time and natural accumulation of dust and mold. But I still think it's a valuable symbol. Confession of sin, our human version of cleansing and cleaning, should not be a source of humiliation or sadness. Yes, feel an appropriate amount of remorse for specific actions that caused harm, and do your best to mend the harm if you can. Accountability and responsibility still matter. But don't despair that you are a terrible person with no hope. To confess your sin is to announce that you remember who you are, where you've been, and where you want to go. That you remember the fundamental beauty of your life and soul. That you desire to face the future armed with lessons learned, and less weighed down by fear.

I love the concept that God is not cleansing you to make you more valuable, but instead He is cleansing you to reveal your true value. You are beautiful to Him. Priceless, in fact. He loves everything about you and wants you to shine. When we understand sin as something that tarnishes us, we also realize it tarnishes the surface, not the essence of who we are. We have been bought with a price, and our intrinsic worth is not in question. "You are not your own; you were bought at a price" (1 Corinthians 6:19–20). You are costly and valuable, and He deems you worth the high, high price He paid. Deep down in the part of you that is spirit, where God dwells by His Spirit, you are perfected by His presence. The fact that He is in residence makes you holy ground. But the part of you that is spirit is encased in a human personality and housed in a body. There is where sin's tarnish camouflages your true beauty.

Pure Silver

God uses the picture of silver to describe His people and of refined silver to illustrate His purifying work: "He will be like a refiner's fire or a launderer's soap. He will sit as a refiner and purifier of silver; he will purify the Levites [priestly tribe; we are now His priests] and refine them like gold and silver" (Malachi 3:2–3).

Why silver? Silver has many qualities that demonstrate what our purified hearts are like.

> Silver is resistant to corrosion from the atmosphere. Atmospheric corrosives cannot destroy silver, but can only produce surface tarnish. A pure heart is resistant to corrosion and corruption by outside influences. "Do not conform any longer to the pattern of this world, but be transformed by the renewing of your mind. Then you will be able to test and approve what God's will is—his good, pleasing and perfect will" (Romans 12:2).
>
> Paul contrasts two ways of changing: conforming and being transformed. The word "conform" means to be changed from the outside or to be squeezed into a mold. The word "transform" means to be changed from within. Both words mean to change forms, but one indicates change from the outside and one from the inside. Paul warns that the world wants to force you into a form that is not a natural fit. God wants to change your outward form so that it fits your inner being. He wants your inward self to be authentically reflected in your personality and lifestyle. His will for you is a perfect fit. The world's pattern is restrictive, diminishing, smothering. His will for you is beneficial and pleasing.

God wants to make you resistant to the forces and elements that would corrode your beauty by trying to conform you to a pattern that does not fit you. He wants you to be forged into His image so that the corrosion in the world will not penetrate your life and diminish you. He will bring this about by renewing your mind—making your mind something different than it was before. Under His influence, you will begin to know, understand, and embrace God's good, pleasing, and perfect will.

Power flows from purity. Seek purity and you will find power. —*Live a Praying Life® Workbook (10th Anniversary Edition)*, p. 145

Sin tarnishes but does not destroy you because you are a new kind of creation. You are of a different substance from what you were before Christ transformed you by His indwelling presence. Sin mars your appearance but not your worth. It clouds your beauty but does not lessen your value.

As you expose your heart to its loving Pursuer, offer it to Him completely. Invite His love to search out and reveal what needs to be cleansed. Name everything He brings to mind. Name it, repent of it, and turn your back on it. Release it to Him for deep cleansing.

Marinate Your Heart

Rest here, in the words of Psalm 139:23–24. Let them sink into you and nest in your heart. Respond.

Search me, God, and know my heart; test me and know my anxious thoughts. See if there is any offensive way in me, and lead me in the way everlasting. —Psalm 139:23–24

DAY 18

In confession and repentance we find relief. When we turn from our sins and from letting our human nature and inclinations take the lead, we begin to find the life for which we were designed. Living in obedience is not restrictive but liberating. Purity opens you to the power God wants to pour through your life. Cleansing makes you available to hear His voice. Holiness fits you.

> As we give ourselves fully to obedience, we must begin in His law. One can view a lawgiver from two perspectives. First, there's the overbearing, power-hungry, demanding authority figure who says, "I'm laying down the law and you have to obey it because I'm the one with the power. I'm establishing a code of behavior that suits me, and I'm expecting you to follow my rules. If you don't, I'll punish you."
>
> This is not God the lawgiver.
>
> Here's God the lawgiver: "I'm the Creator. I made everything that exists. Because I love you, I'm giving you the laws of the universe. I'm telling you how to get the most out of all that I have created for you. I'm telling you the secrets about how things work so that you can live the life you are created for."
>
> God is the lawgiver because God is the Creator.
>
> God's will for you is that you flourish and prosper. His law is your protection and your wisdom. His law is encoded in your spiritual DNA so that in following it you are cooperating in establishing your own fulfillment and success. —*Live a Praying Life® Workbook (10th Anniversary Edition)*, p. 172

He has built His law into our spiritual blueprint. In working against it, we are working against our own best interest. In resisting it, we resist peace and harmony. Outside His law, we are engaged in an ongoing, energy-draining, life-sapping upstream swim. In giving us His law, He has not restricted us but freed us.

I run in the path of your commands, for you have broadened my understanding. . . . . Direct me in the path of your commands, for there I find delight. —Psalm 119:32, 35

The law of the LORD is perfect, refreshing the soul. . . . The precepts of the LORD are right, giving joy to the heart. —Psalm 19:7–8

By them [God's laws] your servant is warned; in keeping them there is great reward. —Psalm 19:11

When He is speaking to your heart from Scripture, His Word acts as a stain detector. When you realize you have stained your clothes, for example, you want to deal with that stain as quickly as possible to keep it from setting. It is to your advantage to have the stain brought to your attention promptly. When you read His Word and your conscience is pricked because you see where you are off course, all you have to do is return. Stop. Confess. Regroup. You are met with the Father's welcome, not His anger. He Himself, through His Spirit Who indwells you, rushes in to empower you for obedience.

Prayer is the avenue upon which the power and provision of God travels from the spiritual realm to the circumstances of earth. It is essential the avenue be unimpeded so power can flow freely.

Marinate Your Heart

Listen for the living voice of the Holy Spirit in the words of Hebrews 4:12–13. Respond.

For the word of God is alive and active. Sharper than any double-edged sword, it penetrates even to dividing soul and spirit, joints and marrow; it judges the thoughts and attitudes of the heart. Nothing in all creation is hidden from God's sight. Everything is uncovered and laid bare before the eyes of him to whom we must give account. —Hebrews 4:12–13

DAY 19

Jesus compared the Word of God to a seed and our hearts to soil. For a seed to grow into a crop, it has to be planted. It has to burrow into the soil so the soil and the seed can interact. The seed has to put down roots before it grows fruit. When the seed and the soil come together, that combination sets off a process.

Jesus told a parable about four kinds of soil. The soil represents our hearts. The condition of the soil determines the harvest of the seed. Jesus told this familiar parable in Mark 4:1–9. No matter what condition the soil is in, the soil can be redeemed. The soil can be transformed. Consider how your heart receives the seed of the Word.

> The farmer Jesus told about encountered several kinds of soil in the field he was sowing. On the surface, all the soil looked the same. The difference only became obvious by the crop it produced. Let's discuss those soils.
>
> **Hard soil:** The sower would walk along paths in the fields as he sowed. The paths were well traveled and the soil was packed down and hard. Some of the seed would fall on these hard paths. The seed could not break through the hard packed soil to put down roots and would be blown away by the wind or simply dry up and die without sprouting.
>
> **Rocky soil:** The farmer encountered rocky ground, such as the sections of limestone covered by three or four inches of earth, as can be found in Palestine. In those places, the roots of the plants could go down only so far. The plants sprouted

upward quickly because growth was upward instead of downward. But because their root systems were shallow, providing inadequate access to water and nutrients in the soil, the plants died very quickly from the heat of the sun. This kind of soil could not be identified simply by looking at it, because on the surface, it looked just fine.

Thorny soil: Some soil had the seeds of weeds in it. The weeds were not visible, but when the sowed seeds began to sprout, the weed seeds sprouted too. The weeds were in their native soil—they owned that ground. These weeds overpowered the good plants.

Good soil: The good soil was deep and rich and ready to receive seed. It had no weeds. The soil was cultivated by the farmer, and the soil had benefited from that cultivation. It was prepared to take the seed in, let it put down deep roots, nourish it, and cause it to grow fruit. . . .

If you were able to identify some areas in your heart that would correspond to each type of undesirable soil, let Jesus show you how each can be transformed into rich soil that grows lush fruit.

Hard soil: I have a friend who came to the LORD as an adult. She has experienced three failed marriages and other dating relationships that turned out badly. Her adult children are hurt and angry with her for the chaos she inflicted on their lives. Before she came to know Jesus, she tried many different paths to find God and was disillusioned each time, usually by the people who claimed to have "the answer" but were really as lost and wandering as she was. It is still very hard for the truth of God's unconditional love and His total forgiveness to penetrate the part of her heart that is packed down because of so much painful traffic. The Father has an answer for my friend. He makes this promise to her: . . . "Who can tip over the water jars of the heavens when the dust becomes hard and the clods of earth stick together?" (Job 38:36–38)

The same One who pours out rain on the earth to soften the hardened soil can pour out the Holy Spirit on your heart right where it is least penetrable and most resistant. He is the One who created those thought and reasoning processes to begin with. He knows how to work in them and through them. Be patient. Let kingdom processes work.

Rocky soil: Another dear friend of mine suffered terrible abuse as a child and was raped as a teenager. She has a boulder of anger covered over with a shallow layer of rich, fertile soil. She loves the Word and receives it gladly and enthusiastically. She never misses an opportunity to hear a famous speaker or writer. She reads all the time. Her embrace of the Word is genuine. But she realizes that while it springs up quickly, it just as quickly fades. Then she has to find a new Bible study, new conference, or new book. My friend has deep spiritual roots in many ways, but the seed that falls on that shallow ground keeps disappointing her. The LORD has a promise for her: "'Is not my word like fire,' declares the LORD, 'and like a hammer that breaks a rock in pieces?'" (Jeremiah 23:29).

The LORD speaks His Word into your life, and it works as a hammer to break that rock in pieces. Maybe you want big and shiny and quick and easy, but the Word that breaks the rock in pieces is slow and steady and strong. Don't keep moving on to the next big thing. Don't keep looking for the book or speaker who will break open that rock. Give the kingdom process time to work.

Thorny soil: . . . Some issues in my life require constant vigilance because their seeds still lie dormant and ready to grow again at any time. I might make a lot of progress, but then, when I feel discouraged or sad or worn out, up pops the weed and chokes out some fruit that was beginning to grow. Some kinds of obedience come right from my heart; in those cases, I find it harder to disobey than to obey. Then other kinds of obedience require effort. The LORD has a promise for me: "I went past the field of the sluggard, past the vineyard of the man who lacks judgment; thorns had come up everywhere, the ground was covered with weeds, and the stone wall was in ruins. I applied my heart to what I observed and learned a lesson from what I saw: A little sleep, a little slumber, a little folding of the hands to rest—and poverty will come on you like a bandit and scarcity like an armed man" (Proverbs 24: 30–34). . . .

As He tells you that weeds grow up where discipline is lacking, He is offering to provide that discipline in you. He is reminding you that where there are weeds, the Word is being choked out. You are missing out on what He has for you. Learn the lesson. Respond! Let the kingdom process work.

Good soil: Your heart is mostly good soil. God has redeemed lots of ground in your life, making it ready to receive the Word and give the Word deep roots. Even good soil has to be prepared. It has to be plowed. When the LORD is turning over the soil in your heart, don't try to pat it all back down and make it nice and even like it used to be. Let the LORD prepare the ground for the seed He wants to plant there. "Break up your unplowed ground" (Jeremiah 4:3). God has a promise for you: "The LORD will guide you always; he will satisfy your needs in a sun-scorched land and will strengthen your frame. You will be like a well-watered garden, like a spring whose waters never fail" (Isaiah 58:11). "The seed will grow

> well, the vine will yield its fruit, the ground will produce its
> crops, and the heavens will drop their dew" (Zechariah 8:12).
> —*Secrets Jesus Shared: Kingdom Insights Revealed through the
> Parables*, pp. 84–89

Let His living Word plant the seeds of righteousness and holiness and purity. Let God do whatever work is necessary to make your heart fertile ground for His Word. Let Him transform the soil of your life so that it is the right environment for the seed to flower.

Marinate Your Heart

Take His Word in. Reflect on every word. Ask the Spirit to unpack its riches. Respond.

For this command is a lamp, this teaching is a light, and correction and instruction are the way to life. —Proverbs 6:23

DAY 20

As you expose your heart to Him and ask Him to reveal the places where sin has found a home, you experience His glad and jubilant forgiveness. He does not offer His forgiveness grudgingly but freely and joyfully. Without hesitation. And He calls on us to forgive others the same way. "Be gentle with one another, sensitive. Forgive one another as quickly and thoroughly as God in Christ forgave you" (Ephesians 4:32 *The Message*).

> Father, You forgive me so freely and so readily. The least infraction meets with Your immediate grace, and the gravest sin is absolved with prepaid atonement. I never have to earn my way back into Your favor. I never have to pay for my sins. I'm not expected to deserve the grace lavished on me. I hate my sins because they no longer fit me. I fear the chaos my sins bring to my life and the interruption of the free flow between You and me. But I don't have to fear Your retribution. I don't have to fear that You will walk away from my life. Empower me to forgive others as You forgive me—freely and readily. —*Conversations With the Most High: 365 Days in God's Presence*, p. 58

To hold on to bitterness and refuse forgiveness is a sin. It is a sin that saps you of joy and robs you of peace. It hobbles your progress and weighs you down. When the Holy Spirit turns His spotlight on your heart, unforgiveness is revealed. I think of the Holy Spirit as saying, "Come out with your hands up!" When He reveals the

places where anger and resentment have been lurking, He calls
them out and demands their surrender. He loves you too much to
let bitterness infect you.

> Child, offspring of My Spirit, bitterness is not at home in
> you. I indwell you, and your life is not the natural environ-
> ment for bitterness to root and grow. It is a weed, a fruit
> destroyer, an invader. It is sapping your joy and stunting
> your growth. Let Me have it, and I will uproot it. Unable to
> receive nourishment, it will wither and die. You will be free.
> Give Me your permission to begin the process. "See to it that
> no one falls short of the grace of God and that no bitter root
> grows up to cause trouble and defile many" (Hebrews 12:15).
> —*Conversations With the Most High: 365 Days in God's
> Presence*, p. 160

Pass It On

Holding on to bitterness and resentment is an affront to the Cross.
Jesus died for the sins of your offender. He died for the wounds
and the hurt inflicted on you by others. The searchlight of His love
will find deposits of anger that are spreading and taking up more
and more room as time goes by. He sees the poison spreading, and
He will not ignore it. Bitterness is toxic. He loves you too much. He
has forgiven you. Pass it on.

> To sync your heart with Jesus' heart, receive His forgiveness
> and then pass it on. Do not refuse to acknowledge sin or for-
> sake sin that the Holy Spirit has identified in you. Refusing
> to accept and receive the forgiveness He paid so high a price
> for you to have will keep you from the full force of His life
> and the total experience of His love for you. It won't lessen
> His love for you, but it will rob you of fully knowing it in

your experience. On the other hand, to hang onto bitterness and anger toward someone who has hurt or offended you will keep you arm's length from His heart—not because He has removed Himself from you, but rather because you have chosen to erect and protect a barrier around your own heart. His command for you to forgive is an invitation to live with your heart synced to His love. —*Synced: Living Connected to the Heart of Jesus*, pp. 157–158

When the Holy Spirit searches your heart, He is doing so for your benefit. He will not let unforgiveness lie in wait, hiding out until the moment comes for an ambush and anger takes over your emotions. You don't even know where it came from. Or you think the anger is brought on by your current situation. But it has been festering in you, resisting His healing touch, ready to pounce at an unexpected moment. You find yourself expressing anger at someone other than the one who truly offended you. Unforgiveness is lethal, nasty, devious. Face it. Name it. Let it go.

Child, I want you free. Every command I give is meant to lead you into more freedom. When I command you to forgive, it is My loving call to you to walk in freedom. Unforgiveness keeps you tied to your past and keeps you tied to your offender. You carry your offender around on your back as a heavy, paralyzing load. When I died for the sins you have committed, I also died for the sins committed against you. Let Me pour My love into your heart. My love is big enough and powerful enough to dissolve anger and resentment— for your sake. "And hope does not put us to shame, because God's love has been poured out into our hearts through the Holy Spirit, who has been given to us" (Romans 5:5). —*Conversations With the Most High: 365 Days in God's Presence*, p. 57

Marinate Your Heart

Let the power of His living Word permeate your heart and mind. Give yourself over to Him and to His great love for you that calls you to release bitterness. Respond.

Therefore, as God's chosen people, holy and dearly loved, clothe yourselves with compassion, kindness, humility, gentleness and patience. Bear with each other and forgive one another if any of you has a grievance against someone. Forgive as the LORD forgave you. And over all these virtues put on love, which binds them all together in perfect unity.
—Colossians 3:12–13

DAY 21

When you begin to see your sins as God sees them, it will lead to repentance. Repentance begins with sorrow. We can't see our sins in the light of truth and not feel sorrow. Our sins have not only hurt us, but they have hurt others. Most of all, they have grieved the heart of God. But here is the decisive moment, the crossroads, the axis upon which the future will turn. The Holy Spirit's convicting presence uncovers those things we thought were buried away. He is wielding the scalpel of His Word—not to wound but to heal. He is loosing the fire of His Word—not to destroy but to cleanse. Give yourself over to Him, and let Him irrigate your wounds and restore your soul.

> At your entrance to the kingdom, when the King comes into your life to rule there, He begins to recreate your heart so that it is the exact reflection of His. Jesus has no sin of His own to mourn over, but He does mourn over your sin. He mourns over your sin because of how deeply He loves you. That which is named by God as "sin" is that which diminishes your life. That's why it is called sin. It hurts you. It causes you harm. It impedes you. Jesus hates sin because Jesus loves you.
>
> When the living, indwelling, present Jesus communicates His heart to you regarding your sin, it is called conviction. Your enemy condemns, but Jesus convicts. Condemnation brings guilt and hopelessness, but conviction brings repentance and restoration. Conviction brings what Paul refers to as

"godly sorrow." "For you became sorrowful as God intended and so were not harmed in any way by us. Godly sorrow brings repentance that leads to salvation and leaves no regret, but worldly sorrow brings death" (2 Corinthians 7:9–11).

Jesus' sorrow over your sin, transfused into your heart, results in repentance. Repentance leads to salvation—not just the initial acceptance of eternal salvation, but continual salvation from the sins that have a grip on you. Each experience of conviction that leads to repentance and then leads to freedom allows you to know the comfort of the Father. The full force of the blood of Christ, flowing through you now, washing away your sins—could there be any greater comfort?
—*Set Apart: A Six-Week Study of the Beatitudes*, p. 73

Our sins give our enemy a foothold from which to manipulate our human nature. He does not possess you. You belong to Jesus. Your enemy is not in you. Jesus will not share space with him. But from outside you, he lies his lies and suggests God is not all He says He is. The mayhem he causes disrupts prayer.

Be responsive to conviction. It is to your benefit. It is for your good.

Ask for the things you need. Bring everything to Him, asking for heaven to intervene on earth. Be vulnerable to His conviction of sin so He can free you of sin's warping influence. Be tender toward those who have hurt and offended you, and respond when the Spirit brings those very ones to mind. Leave your enemy defeated and in the dust by allowing God to keep unmasking his lies and pointing you to the truth.
—*Prayer Fatigue: Ten Ways to Revive Your Prayer Life*, p. 106

Love Overcomes

As we grow in our love for God, sin loses its hold. The key to repentance and cleansing is not simply trying to come up with our sins so we can repent but rather being open to God and loving Him and rejoicing in Him.

> Jesus, fill me so full of Yourself that You take up all the space. Nothing but You. No room for flesh's ways, or sin's pull. All the places of pettiness and selfishness that occupy my life, I surrender them to You for cleansing. Wash me and I will be whiter than snow. . . .
>
> Jesus, the only remedy for my tendency to fall again into sinful behaviors and habits is the all-surpassing beauty of You. Teach me to maximize my pleasure in You. To find my deepest joy in Your presence. As my heart habituates to the beautiful reality of the spiritual realm, and of Your nearness, the appeal of my sins loses its hold. I find myself not sinning in ways I used to, not because of my tremendous willpower, but because sin is losing its luster. What can compare to You? —*Conversations With the Most High: 365 Days in God's Presence*, pp. 59 and 183

Little by little, sin will lose its grip. It will happen. Our sins are rooted in lies we believe—lies about God, lies about ourselves, lies about others, lies about what we need for happiness. Truth trumps lies. The more we immerse ourselves in truth, and the more we live in dynamic relationship with One who is Truth, the more truth rules us.

Marinate Your Heart

Make Psalm 25:4–11 your heartfelt prayer. Put these verses in your own words so they are yours. Respond.

Show me your ways, LORD, teach me your paths. Guide me
in your truth and teach me, for you are God my Savior, and
my hope is in you all day long. Remember, LORD, your great
mercy and love, for they are from of old. Do not remember
the sins of my youth and my rebellious ways; according to
your love remember me, for you, LORD, are good. Good and
upright is the LORD; therefore he instructs sinners in his ways.
He guides the humble in what is right and teaches them his
way. All the ways of the LORD are loving and faithful toward
those who keep the demands of his covenant. For the sake of
your name, LORD, forgive my iniquity, though it is great.
—Psalm 25:4–11

KNOCK

Ask and it will be given to you; seek and you
will find; knock and the door will be opened
to you. For everyone who asks receives; the one
who seeks finds; and to the one who knocks,
the door will be opened. —Matthew 7:7–8

DAY 22

God invites us to ask Him for anything and everything. Nothing is too big and nothing is too small. Asking in prayer is God's design for how we will see His hand at work in our world.

Jesus encouraged us to ask, and in His Sermon on the Mount, He phrased it this way:

> Ask and it will be given to you; seek and you will find; knock and the door will be opened to you. For everyone who asks receives; the one who seeks finds; and to the one who knocks, the door will be opened. —Matthew 7:7–8

Ask

In typical rabbinical style, Jesus said the same thing three different ways. Each different expression of the thought adds to our understanding of it. By taking the time to express it in such detail, Jesus emphasized how important it is for us to grasp. So let's examine each statement to see what He is telling us about coming to God with our every need and desire.

God invites you to draw upon His resources for your daily needs—physical, emotional, or spiritual. God will provide for you in a practical way. He created your earthbound, time-bound frame and is prepared to meet your every need. God does not have a set of resources with fixed limits. His riches cannot be depleted if used too often. He pleads with you to come to Him in every circumstance, and to come again and again. He is never tired of hearing from you and providing for you. He rejoices over you and rejoices in doing good things for you. If something touches you, it touches Him. You are the apple of His eye. He dotes on you and longs to lavish His love and wealth on you. He wants you, by a choice of your free will, to turn to Him and accept all He wants to give. He waits for you to respond to His generosity by asking, seeking, and knocking.

Jesus said, "I tell you the truth, unless you change and become like little children, you will never enter the kingdom of heaven" (Matthew 18:3). To see the kingdom of God clearly, one must leave behind adult pretenses and sophisticated arguments. Often, we come to God prepared to do battle with Him, convince Him of the validity of our need and give Him reasons to meet it.

What a contrast to the way a little child comes to his or her parents. A child simply assumes that the need or desire is potent enough to speak for itself. All that is required is to bring that need to Mom's or Dad's attention. The request assumes the answer. The child's only thought is to bring the need to the source of supply.

You don't need to build a theological case for why God should want to meet your need. He wants to meet your need because He's your daddy and you are the apple of His eye. Jesus highlights the simplicity of supplication by saying, "Ask and it will be given to you. . . . For everyone who asks receives" (Matthew 7:7–8). The Greek word translated "ask" is used to ask for something to be given, not done. It is the simplest, most straightforward picture of asking for something you need.

Jesus elaborates on this principle further in the following verses. "Which of you, if his son asks for bread, will give him a stone? Or if he asks for a fish, will give him a snake? If you, then, though you are evil, know how to give good gifts to your children, how much more will your Father in heaven give good gifts to those who ask him!" (Matthew 7:9–11).

The purest, most unselfish love I have is for my children. For them, I would lay down my life without thinking twice. Their needs are more important than my own. Without flinching, I would make any sacrifice for their happiness. A parent's love for his or her children, in the best of cases, most closely resembles God's love for us. To even begin to understand God's love for us, we would have to take the highest love we know and multiply it by infinity. If you would give good gifts to your children, how much more would God give to His? I don't have to be convinced to give my children what they need. I want to meet their needs. God "richly blesses all who call on him" (Romans 10:12).

Your asking should be anxiety free. "Do not worry about your life" (Matthew 6:25). Jesus tells you that God is aware of your material needs. You can simply ask for your daily needs to be met without having to remind God, and then focus your attention on the kingdom of God and His righteousness. God wants to free you from anxiety about your daily needs so that you will be able to focus on Him. (See Matthew 6:25–34.) —*Heart's Cry: Principles of Prayer*, pp. 97–99

Proof

God wants to prove Himself to you. He set things up so your asking releases His supply. Your requests access all of heaven's power and all of heaven's provision for the circumstances of earth. When your heart is inclined toward God and you are moved to ask, it is God prompting and drawing you. He wants you to know how close He is, how watchful over you, how ready to give.

> Child, beloved, I am watching over you continually. My eye never wanders. I never fall asleep. You are always in My care. You do not have to perform rituals that will attract My attention. You have My full attention every minute of every day. You cannot ask more of Me than I am longing to give. Ask! Ask! And keep on asking! —*Conversations With the Most High: 365 Days in God's Presence*, p. 168

When you ask, you are acknowledging Him as the focus of your faith. You trust His love for you, knowing He delights in providing for you. You trust His power, knowing He has the ability to meet your every need. You trust His wisdom, knowing He knows best when and how to meet your need. He wants you to ask. He invites you to ask. He is honored by your asking.

Marinate Your Heart

Let the Holy Spirit speak the familiar words of Ephesians 3:20 to you in the context of your life and your needs right now. Respond.

> Now to him who is able to do immeasurably more than all we ask or imagine, according to his power that is at work within us. —Ephesians 3:20

DAY 23

Jesus promised that your Father knows what you need before you ask Him. Your asking does not cause Him to suddenly recognize your need. He has your need in mind before you know you have it. Yet in the very same discourse, He instructs us to ask. Let's keep delving into His invitation to ask.

> He has your need in mind before you know you have it.

"Give us today our daily bread" (Matthew 6:11).

The Father wants to meet your needs. He encourages you to look to Him to supply every need that arises. He takes pleasure in supplying you with everything you need.

Why do you have needs? Why do you need shelter or food? Why do you need emotional connections with other people? Why do you need to feel a sense of purpose?

You have needs because God created you with needs. He could have made you so that your shelter is on your back, as He did the turtle. He could have made you so that you could live a solitary, isolated life. But instead, He made you with needs. The reason is so that your needs could be His entry points. Your needs will point you to His supply.

"Meet today's needs," Jesus taught us to pray. "Whatever arises today, Father, I look to You for provision." . . .

What an adventure it is to live this way! How it frees me from anxiety and frustration! I am learning that everything, from the major to the mundane, has been provided for by my Father. As needs arise from day to day, instead of asking, "Father, do something!" I just say, "Father, what have You already done? Where will I discover the answer You have provided? My soul rests in You, waiting patiently for Your salvation."

Please understand, God does not meet every need in the way that seems most convenient to me. If that were my measuring stick, then I would often be frustrated. But if I have given myself to Him as a living offering, then I am open for Him to meet my needs in ways that will further my understanding of Him or will advance His kingdom....

"Ask and it will be given to you . . . For everyone who asks receives" (Matthew 7: 7–8).

Jesus used a very simple form of the word *ask* in this declaration. The phrasing is like a child asking his or her parent to meet a need. Yet Jesus also said, "Your Father knows what you need before you ask him" (Matthew 6: 8). If that's so, why ask?

Let me back up a little. The phrase the Father gave me many years ago to define my message is *the praying life....* A praying life is a life always in active and intentional cooperation with God; a life in which an undercurrent of prayer is always present; a life of continual interaction with the spiritual realm. A praying life is a life open to the power and provision of God....

One of the ways that you open your life to what God wants to provide is by asking! In asking, you acknowledge the Source of everything. "Don't be deceived, my dear brothers. Every good and perfect gift is from above, coming down from the Father of the heavenly lights, who does not change like shifting shadows" (James 1: 16–17). God instructs you to ask for what you need because this interaction keeps you aware that He is your source.

Another reason God designed prayer so that your asking releases His supply is because He wants you to see His power. If His method for meeting your needs did not engage you, you would not see His power at work. He wants you to have observable proof of His involvement in your life; He wants you to see His love for you. . . .

Sometimes God waits for you to ask, because until you see your need, you will not recognize His supply. He waits until you have come to the end of your own resources. He waits for you to turn to Him as the one and only Source. . . .

Peace is yours when you know that He will never withhold from you something that would truly make your life more complete. When you are living in a flow of prayer—a praying life—you can always know: "God will meet my need in the right way at the right time with the right resources. If it is best for my need to be fully met today, then it will be."
—*Set Apart: A Six-Week Study of the Beatitudes*, pp. 160–162

Marinate Your Heart

Consider what each phrase of Psalm 40:5 means to you when it becomes your prayer. Respond.

Many, LORD my God, are the wonders you have done, the things you planned for us. None can compare with you; were I to speak and tell of your deeds, they would be too many to declare. —Psalm 40:5

DAY 24

"Ask and it will be given to you; seek and you will find . . ." To add more layers to our understanding about asking, Jesus next used the word *seek*. In each case—ask, seek, knock—the verb tense is an ongoing action.

> Ask *and* keep on asking and it will be given to you; seek *and* keep on seeking and you will find; knock *and* keep on knocking and the door will be opened to you. For everyone who keeps on asking receives, and he who keeps on seeking finds, and to him who keeps on knocking, it will be opened.
> —Matthew 7:7–8 AMP

Jesus is describing a praying life—a life lived prayerfully. A life lived in interaction with God. A life always watchful for His activity, alert to His promptings. Let's drill down into more of what He is inviting us to when He adds the concept of seeking in prayer.

> Jesus invites you to seek and promises that you will find. For each word—*ask*, *seek*, *knock*—a linear tense is used. This means to ask and keep on asking; seek and keep on seeking; knock and keep on knocking. Seeking prayer is a lifelong quest.
>
> Seeking prayer is different from asking prayer. In seeking prayer, you will be actively involved in a search. The Greek word for *seek* implies to seek something in order to

find and possess it. It does not mean to seek in order to understand or to seek opportunity. What is it that you are to seek?

"But seek first his kingdom and his righteousness, and all these things will be given to you" (Matthew 6:33). Seek the kingdom of God in order to possess it. Everyone who seeks, finds.

The key to seeking prayer is to determine the focus of your search. Jesus tells you that the search for the kingdom of God and His righteousness is a guaranteed reward. This is not a search for divine blessing, or personal gain, or physical comfort. The seeking prayer is: *Father, I want to possess Your kingdom and Your righteousness. I don't want to just know about it. I want it to be mine. I will seek and keep on seeking until I possess every square inch of Your kingdom and every bit of Your righteousness.* . . . The faith for seeking prayer says, *I will have it.* Seeking prayer requires determined faith.

Scripture is the map to guide your search. . . .

As you begin your search, understand that it is God's great desire that you enter and possess His kingdom and His righteousness. "Do not be afraid, little flock, for your Father has been pleased to give you the kingdom" (Luke 12:32). He will not try to hide or disguise it. Seeking prayer will not take you through a labyrinth, but down a straight and narrow road. The way to the kingdom is a person. Jesus said, "I am the way" (John 14:6). The life of Christ flowing through you is the kingdom and righteousness.

The search for the kingdom of God is conducted through prayer. The kingdom is hidden from your physical senses and can only be revealed by the Holy Spirit. "The kingdom of God does not come with your careful observation nor will people say, 'Here it is,' or 'There it is,' because the kingdom of God is within you" (Luke 17:20–21). The kingdom is not experienced physically, but through the Holy Spirit. (See Romans 14:17.)

Seeking prayer brings this attitude to every situation. "Thy kingdom come. Thy will be done on earth as it is in heaven. In every situation, in every person, through every difficulty, establish Your kingdom. Use every situation, every person, every difficulty to give me more of the kingdom, to establish Your righteousness more deeply within me." Through seeking prayer, God will enlighten the eyes of your heart so that you will know the kingdom. —*Heart's Cry: Principles of Prayer*, pp. 99–100

The Kingdom in Action

As we ask, what we are seeking is that the kingdom of God—the rule and authority of Jesus—would be expressed in every need and circumstance. We are offering our petitions as platforms for the display of His power. We are asking Him to show Himself in the middle of our needs and desires.

> To seek requires effort and action on the part of the seeker. What are we to seek? "But seek first his kingdom and his righteousness" (Matthew 6:33*a*). His kingdom and His righteousness are the specific things we are told to seek after. Everything else "will be given to you as well" (Matthew 6: 33*b*). We are to look for, watch for, desire, run after, long for God's kingdom and His righteousness. The kingdom of God is where the will of God is fully present and in effect. How do we seek the kingdom? By deliberate obedience to the King. Every moment that we are in obedience, the kingdom is in effect. When the kingdom is in effect, then the power of God is breaking into the environment of earth. If you

seek, you will find. —*Secrets Jesus Shared: Kingdom Insights Revealed through the Parables*, p. 154

Marinate Your Heart

Focus your whole attention on 2 Chronicles 16:9, and let the Holy Spirit say to you what He wants you to hear today. Respond.

For the eyes of the LORD range throughout the earth to strengthen those whose hearts are fully committed to him. —2 Chronicles 16:9

DAY 25

Ask, seek, knock. Each word gives us a clearer view of what it means to ask God and what is involved in prayer. This method of teaching is like seeing an object from different vantage points. It will be the same object, but you will get a more multidimensional view of it and have a fuller picture. Jesus builds layer upon layer to deepen our understanding of prayer in a few simple sentences.

Knock with Persistent Faith

Jesus illustrated the principle of knocking with a parable. He told a story about a woman badgering an unjust judge until she had received from Him what she needed. Examine this story with me.

Then Jesus told his disciples a parable to show them that they should always pray and not give up. He said: "In a certain town there was a judge who neither feared God nor cared what people thought. And there was a widow in that town who kept coming to him with the plea, 'Grant me justice against my adversary.' For some time he refused. But finally he said to himself, 'Even though I don't fear God or care what people think, yet because this widow keeps bothering me, I will see that she gets justice, so that she won't eventually come and attack me!'" And the LORD said, "Listen to what the unjust judge says. And will not God bring about justice for his chosen ones, who cry out to him day and night? Will he keep putting them off? I tell you, he will see that they get justice, and quickly. However, when the Son of Man comes, will he find faith on the earth?" —Luke 18:1–8

The purpose for this parable is clearly stated. This parable teaches us that we should pray and keep on praying and never give up. Why would Jesus tell a parable with such a specific focus and goal? Obviously He knew that His disciples would have experiences in prayer that would make them want to give up. He knew times would come when prayer would feel like knocking on a door that no one was answering.

Look at the characters Jesus created: two characters from the extreme opposite ends of society's order—the judge and the widow. In Jewish society, the honesty and integrity of a judge was highly valued. The judge had absolute power. He answered to no one. He made decisions about people's lives. The judge who feared neither God nor man was likely a real villain.

A widow was one of society's most defenseless beings.... She had no say. No advocate. She was completely dependent and defenseless. A widow in Palestine of Jesus' day had no voice. She could cry out day and night, and no one had to pay any attention to her. She had no way to stand up for herself.

In this parable, the widow had no resources, and the one who was supposed to be her benefactor and give her provision had become her adversary instead and was keeping provision from her. She came to the unjust judge and kept on coming to him, seeking justice from him. No one expected her, a widow, to come to a judge demanding justice. Her actions were bold and shameless. The Hebrew word Jesus probably used was *chutzpa*—reckless bravery, audacity.

Jesus set up this ludicrous, laughable situation. His listeners probably did laugh when He set the scene. He was being funny, exaggerating to make the picture clear. The widow had a need, and only one person was in a position to move others on her behalf. She knew that only one person had the power to do what she needed to have done.

She kept knocking on his door. She was not dissuaded by the fact that he did not care about her. She did not give up, because she had nowhere else to go. The big, powerful judge, who lived only for himself, was being bothered by a defenseless, powerless widow. The Greek word translated "bothering" is a word used to describe boxing. It means pummeling or assaulting or beating.

Jesus was being witty. He described the imbalance between the two positions, yet used words that meant the little widow was beating up the judge. He didn't mean beating the judge physically, of course. He meant that she was so persistent that she finally wore him out. He gave her what she needed just to get relief from her.

The judge is the opposite of God. Jesus was using the same literary device that we have seen Him use before. If this judge, loathsome as he was, gave the widow what she needed, surely the Father, who loves you, will give you what you need.

Only the judge could move people on the widow's behalf. One of the most exciting and amazing things I have discovered in prayer is that God is able to move other people on your behalf in response to prayer. You can keep your heart and mind focused on Him, and He can move other people to actions and decisions that will accomplish His will for you, just as the judge had the power to compel other people on behalf of the defenseless widow. She didn't keep trying to do battle with her adversaries. She didn't keep trying to manipulate the situation until she got what she wanted. She knew where her answer could be found, and she just kept knocking at that door. —*Secrets Jesus Shared: Kingdom Insights Revealed through the Parables*, pp. 164–165

Your Only Source

Again, Jesus is showing us that when we ask in prayer, we are looking to God as our only source. Whether our needs and desires are physical, financial, emotional, relational, or spiritual, God is the one with the answer. God is the one with the power. God is the one with the provision. Come to Him and don't be dissuaded or discouraged. When it feels as though you are knocking at a door no one is answering, realize Jesus told this parable to encourage you that your answer is coming.

Child, I'm here. I'm ready. Just turn to Me. Everything is ready and waiting. Seeking Me is never in vain. If I am drawing you to Me in the midst of your longing, it is because I have what you need. Everything you need is right here in My hand, and My hand is held out to you. I long to give. I long to bless. I delight in lavishing you with My love, entering right into your messy circumstances, wading into your deep waters. My hands are full of heaven's riches. —*Conversations With the Most High: 365 Days in God's Presence*, p. 168

Marinate Your Heart

Let every word and every phrase of Psalm 69:13 unfold a deeper view of God's heart toward you. Respond.

But I pray to you, LORD, in the time of your favor; in your great love, O God, answer me with your sure salvation. —Psalm 69:13

DAY 26

When we ask, seek, and knock, we engage in a process during which we are changed. Prayer is more than a way to get God to give you things or do things for you. Prayer is how you open your life fully to God for His purposes. We give Him access to every detail of our lives and every facet of our personalities and every thought or idea or emotion. Prayer keeps us positioned where heaven's power flows.

> He wants your experience in prayer to cement for you how trustworthy He is, how faithful He is, how powerful He is.

God is drawing us to prayer. He is pulling us into the orbit of His activity in our lives and in our world. He wants your experience in prayer to cement for you how trustworthy He is, how faithful He is, how powerful He is. He wants you to pray about things big and small.

God is working out the big picture, but He is working it out in the details of life. He invites both macropraying (for big stuff) and micropraying (for smaller details). One of the ways that God teaches us that we can trust Him in the big things is to show us we can trust Him in the small things.

Jesus goes to great lengths to help us see how carefully we are cared for. He makes the point that God is in the very smallest details, so let that lead you to the conclusion that you can trust Him in the big events of life. "Are not two sparrows sold for a penny? Yet not one of them will fall to the ground outside your Father's care. And even the very hairs of your head are all numbered. So don't be afraid; you are worth more than many sparrows" (Matthew 10:29–31).

"Look at the birds of the air; they do not sow or reap or store away in barns, and yet your heavenly Father feeds them. Are you not much more valuable than they? Can any one of you by worrying add a single hour to your life? And why do you worry about clothes? See how the flowers of the field grow. They do not labor or spin. Yet I tell you that not even Solomon in all his splendor was dressed like one of these. If that is how God clothes the grass of the field, which is here today and tomorrow is thrown into the fire, will he not much more clothe you—you of little faith?" (Matthew 6:26–30).

Jesus thinks it is important for His listeners to grasp this. God is at work on the micro level.

Micropraying: Try an experiment. On purpose, give details of your day to God as they come up. This is my very grand prayer as I move through the details of my day: "Here, God." I'm not suggesting that you try to tell God how to smooth out your day or how to manage your life. Just, "Here, God." See what happens. He wants to show you Himself in the small, everyday details so that you will know you can trust Him in the big things. It's training ground. You are not monopolizing God's attention or distracting Him from more important things. He can do everything all the time at full power.

Macropraying: While you're getting the hang of micropraying, learn about macropraying. While God has His fingerprints all over the details, the big things are taking shape. Nothing is too big a prayer. Nothing is too big a cause. Ask big. Then stand back and watch Him move. Slowly, maybe. Incrementally, probably. But move He will, and the timing will be spot on.
—*Prayer Fatigue: Ten Ways to Revive Your Prayer Life,* pp. 154–156

Not a *prayer life*—where some things are fodder for prayer and others are for you to figure out—but a *praying life*. Nothing is too trivial for God's attention, and nothing is asking too much.

Just remember that God answers prayer, but He does not take orders. In our asking, we are releasing. We are handing over our need to Him to unfold His plan. When we think the result of prayer is for God to hand over what we have decided is best, then prayer will often be a disappointing experience. We will have what I call a "prayer list prayer life."

> What do I mean by a prayer list prayer life? This is a mind-set that limits prayer to getting God to perform for you. Understand, there's nothing wrong with a prayer list. In fact, a prayer list is a wonderful tool for observing God's power. It all depends on how you use it. The problem occurs when your prayer list is really a "To Do List" for God. . . .
>
> A "prayer list prayer life" begins to build a distorted understanding of prayer. According to the prayer list, sometimes God says yes and sometimes God says no. Since the praying person would have no way of knowing whether this is a time when God will say yes, or this is a time when God will say no, it becomes very hard to pray boldly and confidently.
>
> As you are learning to live a praying life, prayer takes on a much broader definition than "saying prayers." Much of what prayer is accomplishing cannot be condensed to a list. Many times the direct answers to petitions are the least important aspect of what the prayer accomplished. I believe that as you progress and mature into a praying life, your testimony of prayer's effectiveness will be that the mercies of God unfold at every turn. You walk in answered prayer.

O. Hallesby states it like this: "The longer you live a life of this kind, the more answers to prayer you will experience. As white snow flakes fall quietly and thickly on a winter's day, answers to prayer will settle down on you at every step you take, even to your dying day."

Prayer lists are effective if they are in the context of a praying life. Use your prayer list like this: Write down the concern or the need and date it. The date is the day you surrendered it to God for His purposes, His ways, and His timing. Now, don't watch to see *if* God answers; watch to see *how* God answers. You will find that He answers progressively. He puts together pieces, each one building on the other. Record things as you go along and watch with amazement as God pieces things together for an outcome that is more than you could think or imagine. —*Live a Praying Life® Workbook (10th Anniversary Edition)*, pp. 74–75

Marinate Your Heart

Let the words of Psalm 5:3 frame your prayer. See how your prayer changes. Respond.

In the morning, Lord, you hear my voice; in the morning I lay my requests before you and wait expectantly. —Psalm 5:3

DAY 27

When we ask in prayer, we are reaching into the heavenly realms, taking hold of the power and provision of God and moving it into the circumstances of earth. Prayer is a force that accesses all the power of heaven for the affairs of earth.

> Prayer releases onto the earth what God has prepared in heaven. The answer is prepared before the request is made. In fact, the answer is prepared before the need occurs. "Before they call I will answer; while they are still speaking I will hear" (Isaiah 65:24).
>
> God wants to author our prayers in such a way that He will be glorified. Psalm 50:15 says, "Call to me in the day of trouble; I will deliver you, and you will honor me." When we call to Him, releasing His power and His will, He will be able to bring honor to Himself. He wants our lives to become billboards upon which He can advertise Himself. He wants our lives to be stages upon which He can perform. He wants our lives to be trophy cases in which He can display His mighty deeds. He wants us to be living proof of Him. Through prayer we give Him permission to act in our lives in a way that will show His power and authority.
>
> God wants to do more than you can imagine. Do you really want to limit God to what you can think up? If we could get God to do what we think He should do when we think He should do it, we would miss the eternal plan that exceeds our imaginations.

Consider the story of Lazarus in John 11. Lazarus was
very ill, on his deathbed, and Mary and Martha sent an
urgent message to Jesus: "The one you love is sick." The
implication in their message, and their expectation, was
that Jesus should quickly make His way to Bethany and heal
Lazarus before he died. Jesus did not act in accordance with
their expectations of Him. He did not hurry to Bethany to
heal Lazarus before he died.

Four days elapsed between the time that Lazarus died
and the time that Jesus arrived. You can imagine what a dev-
astating four days it was. Imagine the disillusionment and
disappointment Mary and Martha felt when Jesus failed
to meet their expectations. Everything they believed about
Jesus at that moment was threatened. Have you ever been in
that state? Have you ever been in a situation that, after looking at all the empirical evidence and all the facts, the only
conclusion you could reach was that God had let you down?
That's where Mary and Martha were. They were experiencing a crisis of faith.

Let's look at Mary's and Martha's faith. Both expressed
their firm belief that if Jesus had been there, Lazarus would
not have died (vv. 21, 32). They thought that in asking Jesus
to heal Lazarus, they had asked all that it was possible to ask.
They thought that healing Lazarus was pushing the limits of
His power. Once Lazarus was dead, they reasoned, Jesus was
too late. They had asked all that they could think or imagine.

What did Jesus plan to do? He planned to do more
than they could think or imagine. He was not interested
in meeting their expectations because He intended to
exceed their expectations. He did not confirm their faith,
because He wanted to stretch their faith. He was not content to leave Mary and Martha with what they knew of
Him so far. By raising Lazarus from the dead, He enlarged

their understanding of Him and their view of His power.
When God has access to our needs, He will always show
us something new about Himself. We will learn to align
ourselves with eternal realities and not have our faith sab-
otaged by time-bound, earth-bound vision. We will begin
to live beyond our limits. —*Live a Praying Life® Workbook
(10th Anniversary Edition)*, pp. 68–69

Prayer releases power. Prayer does not give God new ideas or
awaken in Him desires He has not already felt. Prayer is not meant
to convince God of something or wrest tightly
held blessings from His hands. Prayer is a coop-
erative venture with God. Prayer is taking hold
of what He is offering.

> Prayer is taking
> hold of what He
> is offering.

When we believe prayer requires we think up what God should
do and then talk Him into doing it, prayer will never become for
us what God intends. Asking, seeking, knocking shows us there is
more to prayer than placing orders with a divine warehouse and
expecting them to be filled in a timely manner.

Through prayer, we escape our time-bound thinking to par-
ticipate in eternity. We cooperate with God in bringing His power
and provision to bear on lives and situations. Prayer is not a for-
mula, but a life; not a method, but a relationship. When we narrow
prayer's reach to our own best ideas, we often miss what God is
doing.

Child, don't frontload your prayers with your expectations
of what I should do. I have not pledged Myself to your best
idea. I have pledged Myself to more than you could ask or
imagine. When you try to decide for Me how to handle a
situation, you will have your focus on the very narrowly

drawn window of your anticipated answer, and you will miss what I'm doing. Those who were watching for the grand entrance of a mighty king as Messiah, missed the quiet birth in a stable. —*Conversations with the Most High: 365 Days in God's Presence*, p. 206

Marinate Your Heart

As you consider the requests, consider them in light of the truth of 1 Corinthians 2:9.

"What no eye has seen, what no ear has heard, and what no human mind has conceived"—the things God has prepared for those who love him. —1 Corinthians 2:9

DAY 28

God has designed prayer so it releases all His power and in such a way that it deepens our understanding of His ways and cements our hearts to His. A praying life is a life actively engaged with the heavenly realms all day every day.

Prayer is not always formulated in words and sentences. Prayer is always rising from our hearts, and God hears it as though it were perfectly articulated.

> If a praying life is a life open to God, and if we begin to live with our spiritual senses alert to the spiritual realm, it will require a fully devoted heart. . . . With the Holy Spirit as your guide, you will discover a deeper level of living and responding. . . . It will become your soul's habit to turn every thought toward God.
>
> Your mind is an amazing creation. It functions efficiently on many levels at once. It is the ultimate multitasking software. At one time you may be driving a car, remembering directions, carrying on a conversation, retaining a grocery list in your memory, observing the time, and on and on and on. There are mental processes going on that you are not even aware of. Consider this: At one of those levels, prayer is always going on. This is true because the Spirit of Christ lives in you, and He is always praying. Sometimes, prayer is at the most conscious and aware level of thought. Other times it is down a level or two. Once I realized that, it became easier and more natural for me to switch back and forth—to

bring prayer back to the higher awareness level more often and more spontaneously. The reason is that I don't always feel like I'm starting over. I realize that I'm in a continuous flow of prayer. I didn't stop praying, start doing something else, then start praying all over again. The sweet aroma of prayer is always rising from your innermost being before the throne.

Psalm 139:4 says, "Before a word is on my tongue you know it completely, O Lord." Before a need or desire has reached a level of conscious understanding at which you can put it into words—while it is still unformed and raw—God already knows it fully. In Romans 8:26–27, we read, "The Spirit himself intercedes for us with groans that words cannot express. And he who searches our hearts knows the mind of the Spirit, because the Spirit intercedes for the saints in accordance with God's will."

When a desire is nothing but an inarticulate groan— before you can form it into sentences—the Spirit of God is already speaking it with perfect clarity. By the time you begin to speak your need or desire in prayer, you are simply joining into a flow of prayer that is already in progress. "Before they call I will answer; while they are still speaking I will hear" (Isaiah 65:24). —*Live a Praying Life® Workbook (10th Anniversary Edition)*, p. 43

God is not so much a lip reader as He is a heart reader. Your heart's cry is always in His ears. Never is there a moment when you do not have His full, undivided attention. He can give His full and undivided attention to every one of His children without neglecting anyone or anything else. His heart is set on you.

He responds to your requests. He invites and welcomes your petitions. Ask, and keep on asking; seek, and keep on seeking; knock, and keep on knocking.

Marinate Your Heart

Let the words of Psalm 28:6–7 be your prayer.

Blessed be the LORD, because He has heard the voice of my supplications! The LORD is my strength and my shield; my heart trusted in Him, and I am helped; therefore my heart rejoices, and with my song I will praise Him.
—Psalm 28:6–7 NKJV

CONCLUSION

It is my prayer that these twenty-eight days have been a catalyst for deepening your heart's connection with the LORD and launching you into a continued journey to know more and more of Him.

I pray you will progress in the adventure of prayer, depending on the indwelling Jesus to lead you in His paths. I pray that you will grow in boldness and audacity and become an outrageous asker, that you will keep your life open to the activity of the kingdom and the voice of the Spirit.

Have you taken this twenty-eight-day journey with others? Stay connected. Encourage one another in prayer. Share each other's God-adventures.

Keep seeking!

Jennifer

Find resources to help you live a praying life at prayinglife.org.

**If you enjoyed this book, will you consider sharing
the message with others?**

Let us know your thoughts at info@newhopepublishers.com. You
can also let the author know by visiting or sharing a photo of the
cover on our social media pages or leaving a review at a retailer's site.
All of it helps us get the message out!

Twitter.com/NewHopeBooks

Facebook.com/NewHopePublishers

Instagram.com/NewHopePublishers

———————

New Hope® Publishers is an imprint of Iron Stream Media,
which derives its name from Proverbs 27:17,
"As iron sharpens iron, so one person sharpens another."

This sharpening describes the process of discipleship, one to another.
With this in mind, Iron Stream Media provides a variety of solutions
for churches, missionaries, and nonprofits ranging from in-depth
Bible study curriculum and Christian book publishing to custom
publishing and consultative services. Through the popular Life Bible
Study and Student Life Bible Study brands, ISM provides web-based
full-year and short-term Bible study teaching plans as well as printed
devotionals, Bibles, and discipleship curriculum.

For more information on ISM and New Hope Publishers, please visit

IronStreamMedia.com

NewHopePublishers.com

MORE BOOKS BY JENNIFER KENNEDY DEAN

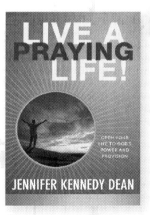
VISIT **NEWHOPEPUBLISHERS.COM**
FOR MORE INFORMATION.